Female Entrepreneurship

Female entrepreneurship, and, in particular, the contribution of their ventures to aggregate economic activity, has gained increasing attention over recent years in terms of theory, practice and policy. This concise book explores how women fit into the contemporary entrepreneurial discourse by recognising that gender intersects with, and influences, women's experience of entrepreneurship.

The book is novel in that it considers women to be a heterogeneous group and as such acknowledges that ethnicity, culture, class and education will all influence and intersect with female entrepreneurship. As a consequence, it explores issues ranging from theoretical relationships between the constructs of gender and entrepreneurship to more empirical work on how entrepreneurship might act as an empowering change agent for women. In order to address the Euro–US-centric assumptions underpinning the influence of gender upon entrepreneurship, a chapter is dedicated to the role of entrepreneurship in empowering Palestine women.

This book will be important supplementary reading on entrepreneurship, small business management and women's/gender studies courses – it will prove particularly useful to women moving towards starting their own business as well as postgraduate students researching the topic for the first time.

Maura McAdam is Senior Lecturer in Management at Queen's University Belfast, UK. She is an Editorial Board Member of the *International Small Business Journal* (ISBJ), as well as an invited Fellow of the Royal Society of Arts (FRSA) and elected Board Member of ISBE (Institute for Small Business and Entrepreneurship). Maura has a broad practical foundation from her work in industry prior to entering academia.

Routledge-ISBE Masters in Entrepreneurship
Edited by Colette Henry and Susan Marlow

The **Routledge-ISBE Masters in Entrepreneurship** series offers postgraduate students specialist but accessible textbooks on a range of entrepreneurship topics. Collectively, these texts form a significant resource base for those studying entrepreneurship, whether as part of an entrepreneurship-related programme of study, or as a new, non-cognate area for students in disciplines such as science and engineering, helping them to gain an in-depth understanding of contemporary entrepreneurial concepts.

The volumes in this series are authored by leading specialists in their field, and although they are discrete texts in their treatment of individual topics, all are united by a common structure and pedagogical approach. Key features of each volume include:

- A critical approach to combining theory with practice, which educates its reader rather than solely teaching a set of skills
- Clear learning objectives for each chapter
- The use of figures, tables and boxes to highlight key ideas, concepts and skills
- An annotated bibliography, guiding students in their further reading, and
- Discussion questions for each chapter to aid learning and put key concepts into practice.

Entrepreneurship
A global perspective
Stephen Roper

Female Entrepreneurship
Maura McAdam

Female Entrepreneurship

Maura McAdam

Routledge
Taylor & Francis Group

LONDON AND NEW YORK

First published 2013
by Routledge
2 Park Square, Milton Park, Abingdon, Oxon OX14 4RN

Simultaneously published in the USA and Canada
by Routledge
711 Third Avenue, New York, NY 10017

Routledge is an imprint of the Taylor & Francis Group, an informa business

British Library Cataloguing in Publication Data
A catalogue record for this book is available from the British Library

Library of Congress Cataloging in Publication Data
McAdam, Maura.
Female entrepreneurship / Maura McAdam.
p. cm.—(Routledge-ISBE masters in entrepreneurship)
Includes bibliographical references and index.
1. Self-employed women. 2. Businesswomen. 3. Women-owned
business enterprises. 4. Entrepreneurship. I. Title.
HD6072.5.M37 2012
338′04082—dc23
2012025387

ISBN: 978-0-415-67819-3 (hbk)
ISBN: 978-0-415-67820-9 (pbk)
ISBN: 978-0-203-07548-7 (ebk)

Typeset in Perpetua and Bell Gothic
by Book Now Ltd, London

Printed and bound in Great Britain by the MPG Books Group

Contents

Figures, tables and boxes

FIGURES

TABLES

BOXES

Series editors' foreword

FEMALE ENTREPRENEURSHIP

It is agreed that entrepreneurial activities and new venture creation are the life-blood of market economies. Yet, for many years the default role model of the entrepreneur was captured in the persona of the 'small business man': a misno-mer suggesting that only men could be recognised as legitimate entrepreneurs. This gender-biased and gender-blind approach has defined this field of research, policy and practice until very recently. In 1989, Holmquist and Sundin summed this up with their apposite observation that small firm research was 'about men, for men and by men'. Since then, a growing body of work has recognised that gen-der is a critical factor within the entrepreneurial field as it shapes our understand-ing of who and what can be legitimately recognised as an entrepreneur. Indeed, the extant literature on female entrepreneurship shows a fascinating thread of development, which, somewhat paradoxically expanded in the 1990s by recognis-ing the role and position of women in this discourse, whilst at the same time mea-suring their contribution against an assumed masculine norm. In essence, a case of 'one step forward' (there are women in this debate) and 'two steps back' (why can they not be, or indeed, how can we make them, more like men?) as gender was utilised as a variable to first, identify female shortcomings in entrepreneurial activ-ities, and second, advance suggestions to repair such 'deficit'. Since then, the debate has progressed significantly to move from reshaping women to be facsi-miles of their male counterparts to the development of a theoretically informed critique of the influence of gender on entrepreneuring. Perhaps one of the most interesting and challenging aspects to emerge from this debate is the lack of performance differences between male- and female-owned firms when all other variables are equally weighted. As such, despite many years of assuming there is something wrong with women's entrepreneurial orientation and attitude, we find it is more likely to be their socio-economic positioning which places them at a dis-advantage. This is a critical point as it suggests that despite the individual neo-liberal discourse surrounding entrepreneurship, premised upon an agentic field of potential realisation, gendered institutional constraints shape and limit women's activities. Thus, gender theory not only exposes how women are subordinated within the prevailing discourse, but also acts as an analytical tool to critique the very idea of entrepreneurship as an individualised emancipatory force.

This text, the second volume in the Routledge-ISBE Masters in Entrepreneurship Series, offers an excellent synopsis of such arguments, providing the reader with an overview of how the research agenda on female entrepreneurship has developed in recent years, how the debate has been shaped by context and drawing implications for future theory development. Consequently, the chapters cover a range of topics within the female entrepreneurship discourse, commencing with a consideration of the definitional issues associated with the study of women entrepreneurs, followed by a consideration of the various socio-economic contexts in which women entrepreneurs operate and the gendered nature of entrepreneurship itself. Throughout the text, students are constantly encouraged to critically evaluate the various theoretical and empirical perspectives presented in the book, and this is reinforced with discussion questions at the end of each chapter. Furthermore, students are encouraged to respond to contemporary calls to embed feminist analyses within entrepreneurial fields of inquiry.

The chapters covering the role of women in family business, non-financial entrepreneurial capital and high technology entrepreneurship offer contemporary feminist perspectives on the female entrepreneurial endeavour, challenging current thinking and pushing the boundaries established in prior literatures. Finally, reflecting on the current state of female entrepreneurship scholarship, and consistent with the book's objective of challenging the prevailing heteronormativity regarding who can be an entrepreneur, the concluding chapter by Professor Susan Marlow offers some new directions for future lines of enquiry while calling for 'ongoing critique' of contemporary and future debates.

Colette Henry and Susan Marlow, June 2012

Acknowledgements

My thanks are due to my dear friend Professor Susan Marlow for providing me with the initial push and continued support to complete this book; and to my Entrepreneurship Class of 2011–12, who unknowingly acted as guinea pigs and helped with the streamlining of ideas presented within it. Finally, this book is dedicated to my mum, whose unconditional love and support never ceases to amaze me.

Chapter 1

Setting the scene

1.1 INTRODUCTION

This chapter presents an overview of the content of the book and its objectives. It sets the whole book in context and provides a basis for the issues, themes and subject matter presented throughout the text. Female entrepreneurship has gained increasing attention over recent years in terms of theory, practice and policy with women's contribution to the growth process of a country widely recognised. As this extant body of evidence has developed, greater focus has been afforded to how gender shapes our understanding of entrepreneurial activity, particularly in respect to the embedded masculinity of the normative model of entrepreneurship. Consequently, this book aims to challenge the prevailing heteronormativity within contemporary assumptions regarding who or what is an entrepreneur through an exploration of how women fit into the contemporary entrepreneurial discourse. It is useful for those wanting to gain an overview of the area as well as those wanting to deepen their knowledge of a specific topic within each chapter.

As a research area, female entrepreneurship is still relativity young (Minniti, 2009). Indeed, the first academic paper which represented the start of a stream of research detailing women's experiences of business ownership was published in 1976 in the *Journal of Contemporary Business* and was called 'Entrepreneurship: A new female frontier' by Eleanor Schwartz. Although not the first on entrepreneurship, it was the first academic paper which focused on female entrepreneurs (Greene *et al.*, 1997). Prior to this entrepreneurship was considered to be a gender neutral concept (Bruni *et al.*, 2004a) with the term entrepreneur referring to a generic creature (De Bruin *et al.*, 2006). In sharp contrast, this book argues that 'the landscape of women's entrepreneurship is a gendered terrain' (Brush *et al.*, 2009: 18) and as such it is no longer appropriate to use the 'male' as the benchmark against which female-owned businesses are measured (Ahl, 2004, 2006). Moreover, this book considers women to be a heterogeneous group and as such acknowledges that ethnicity, culture, class and education will all influence and intersect with women's experiences of business ownership. However, it would be unrealistic to provide a composite account of global female entrepreneurship per se, thus this book predominately focuses upon the experiences of UK, European and North American female entrepreneurs.

1.2 STATEMENT OF AIMS

The key aims of the book are:

1　To explore the socio-economic context for female entrepreneurship in regional, national and international economies.
2　To encourage students to critically evaluate theoretical perspectives on entrepreneurship and their validity with regards to the study of female entrepreneurship.
3　To respond to contemporary calls to embed feminist analyses within the entrepreneurial field of enquiry.

1.3 FEMALE ENTREPRENEURSHIP DEFINED

The aim of this book is to provide insights into female entrepreneurship and begins from the starting point that a woman is 'not a man' or 'the opposite of man' and vice versa (Gherardi, 1995) and so acknowledgement is made with regards to gender differences in entrepreneurial activity (Gatewood *et al.*, 2003; Reynolds *et al.*, 2004). In keeping with the title of the book, we are interested in those businesses created and managed by women. However, definitions of such differ across geographical contexts, thus making direct comparisons difficult. So, for example, in the United Kingdom, a women-owned business is 'one that is either wholly or majority owned by one or more women' (Marlow *et al.*, 2008: 339). Whilst in the United States a 'women-owned business is one in which the principal owner or the majority of shareholders are female, and the female owners/shareholders[1] own at least 51% of the business' (US Census Bureau, 2002: 226). Although similar, both definitions fail to take into account the composite contribution of women to business ownership which is particularly significant in the context of family business.[2] In light of this, the Center for Women's Business Research (CWBR) in the United States differentiates between women-led businesses and women-owned businesses in an attempt to take into account those ventures equally owned by male and female business partners including copreneurial ventures.

1.4 BEFORE WE START – A FEW STATISTICS

As the number of women-owned businesses increases, their performance and in particular their contribution to aggregate economic activity had gained increasing

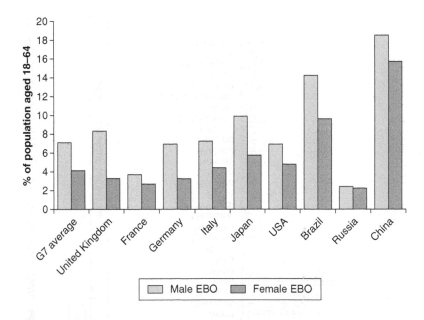

Figure 1.1

Established business ownership by gender in participating G7 and BRIC countries, 2009

Source: GEM 2009 APS (see www.gemconsortium.org).

importance (Watson, 2002; Allen *et al.*, 2007; Naude and Van der Walt, 2008). Although not engaged at the same rate as their male equivalents[3], women world-wide are actively engaged in entrepreneurial activity (de Bruin *et al.*, 2006) with female entrepreneurial activity representing 'an increasingly important part of the economic profile of any country' (Allen *et al.*, 2007: 9). However, despite this, on average men are twice as likely as women to be in the process of launching a new venture which is persistent and consistent across countries (Reynolds *et al.*, 2002; Acs *et al.*, 2005).

Figure 1.1 demonstrates that the differences between men and women are remarkably stable across countries. However, it is important to note, that locality matters (Hill *et al.*, 2006) and as a result there are regional variations when it comes to entrepreneurial activity amongst women.

As can be seen from Figure 1.2, Ghana is the only country where women are more active in entrepreneurship than men (GEM, 2009; Minniti, 2009). According to GEM (2009), regardless of country, education attainment, work status and income, women tend to be less confident and more pessimistic when compared to their male counterparts.

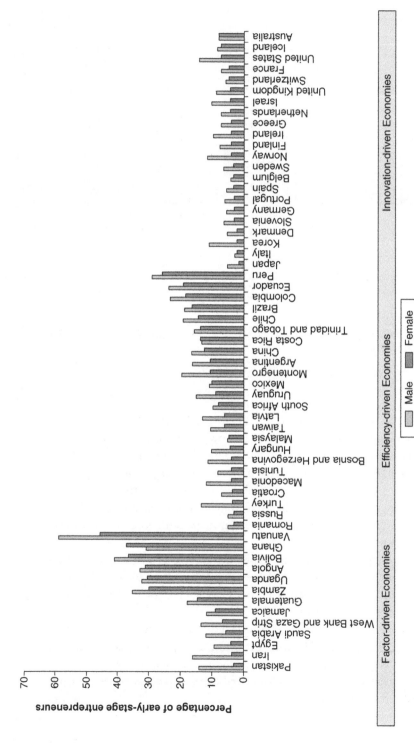

Figure 1.2
GEM economies ranked by level of female participation in total early-stage entrepreneurship activity (TEA) by economic group, 2010

Source: GEM Adult Population Survey (APS) (see www.gemconsortium.org).

1.5 THE LURE OF BUSINESS OWNERSHIP

As well as the desire for flexibility, job satisfaction and quality of life have also been identified as significant in the entrepreneurial decisions made by women (Shabbir and Di Gregorio, 1996). However, it is important to note that business ownership is not necessarily a solution for work–life balance challenges, and in fact, female entrepreneurs still experience some degrees of family–work conflict (Shelton, 2006). Entrepreneurship is often lauded as the solution for those women who have been pushed out of corporate employment due to frustration, discontentment and discrimination (Heilman and Chen, 2003). As such, enterprise is seen as an outlet for women deciding to leave dependent employment in organisations where they have experienced a lack of opportunities for advancement (Marlow and McAdam, 2012) as 'entrepreneurship holds the promise that individuals' career success will rise or fall on their own merit' (Heilman and Chen, 2003: 360). However, the perception of entrepreneurship as a solution to the glass ceiling effect only 'reinforces a social order where men support men in a homosocial pattern and acknowledges the discrimination of women in the corporate ladders' (Ahl, 2004: 177). Self-employment may, in fact, not be the solution to discriminatory advancement issues or frustration problems experienced in the labour market; some of this may actually follow women into self-employment.

1.6 PROFILE OF WOMEN-OWNED BUSINESSES

As noted, the presence of women in entrepreneurial careers remains low; furthermore, these ventures are overly concentrated in crowded, low value added sectors (Marlow et al., 2008) with the majority of women-owned businesses in the retail, catering and health/education service sectors. As a consequence, women's preferences for flexibility and the prioritisation of household production (Parker, 2009) may result in them being drawn towards industrial sectors where entry and capital costs are low and where flexibility and work–life balance is easily achieved (Hundley, 2001a). However, service and retail services are highly competitive, with limited opportunities for growth and profitability (Kalleberg and Leicht, 1991; Coleman, 2007). In fact, such sectors yield lower returns than sectors such as technology where male businesses dominate (Allen et al., 2007).

Although there are many similarities in the operating profiles of small firms despite the characteristics of the owner, the operating profiles of female-owned firms do exhibit feminised working patterns; the available data indicates that around half of self-employed women work part-time (less than 30 hours per week) and around a third base their businesses within the home (Ahl, 2004). Women adopt such operating profiles in an effort to combine economic activity, domestic labour and childcare (Belle and La Valle, 2003; Rouse and Kitching, 2006). While such fragmented approaches to business operation may be a rational

5

Table 1.1 *The classifications of a typical female entrepreneur*

The 'aimless' young women who set up a business essentially as an alternative to unemployment.

The 'success-oriented' young women for whom entrepreneurship is not a more or less random or obligatory choice but a long-term career strategy.

The 'strongly success-oriented' women, usually without children, who view entrepreneurial activity as an opportunity for greater professional fulfilment or as a means to overcome the obstacles against career advancement encountered in the organisations for which they previously worked.

The 'dualists', often with substantial work experience, who must reconcile work and family responsibilities and are therefore looking for a solution which gives them flexibility.

The 'return workers', or workers (usually low-skilled) who have quit their previous jobs to look after their families and are motivated by mainly economic considerations or by a desire to create space for self-fulfilment outside the family sphere.

The 'traditionalists', or women with family backgrounds in which owning and running a business is a longstanding tradition.

The 'radicals', or women motivated by a culture antagonist to conventional entrepreneurial values, who set up initiatives intended to promote the interests of women in society.

Source: Bruni *et al.* (2004a: 261–262).

response to the positioning of self-employed women in a particular socio-economic context, they may have a negative effect on the normative credibility of the business and the business owner (Marlow and McAdam, 2012).

1.7 TYPOLOGY OF FEMALE ENTREPRENEURS

Numerous attempts have been made to construct a typology of female entrepreneurs (Goffee and Scase, 1985; Cromie and Hayes, 1988; Monaci, 1997). Bruni *et al.* (2004a: 261–262) merge the key categories which result in the classifications of a typical female entrepreneur as set out in Table 1.1.

Starting a business regardless of gender is a complex issue (Langowitz and Minniti, 2007); however, there is evidence to suggest that the decision may be more complicated for women due to their sensitivity to non-monetary factors (Bird and Brush, 2002). It is evident from the above classifications that women's reproductive life cycle plays an influential role in their entrepreneurial decisions; with the private and public spheres intertwined (Bruni *et al.*, 2004a). This will be explored further in Chapter 5.

1.8 BOOK STRUCTURE

Chapter 2 commences with an exploration of the socio-economic context for female entrepreneurship in order to provide an understanding of the socialisation processes that inform women's decision making when it comes to entrepreneurial activity. Then, in Chapter 3, the so-called gender neutrality of entrepreneurship is challenged in order to expose the androcentric nature of the entrepreneurial discourse. Furthermore, the challenges this poses for women with regards fit and credibility within entrepreneuring is discussed. Thus, a conceptual framework is required which takes into account feminism and gender; consequently Chapter 4 considers the contribution of feminist theory in illuminating women's experiences of entrepreneurial activity. As already noted, the family is an important influencing factor on women's ability and willingness to engage with entrepreneurial activity. Furthermore, it would be an oversight not to acknowledge women's contribution to the area of family business. Therefore, the intersection of the business and family domains are explored in Chapter 5. Regardless of geographical context, entrepreneurs draw upon a broad and deep range of financial, human, social and symbolic capital to create and grow sustainable ventures. However, the nature and composition of entrepreneurial capital differs with gender. In Chapter 6 the non-financial aspects of entrepreneurial capital accrual are discussed whilst the challenges faced by women when it comes to financing their ventures is addressed in Chapter 7. Women-owned businesses are traditionally found and associated with sectors such as health, catering, caring and personal services. However, there is evidence to suggest that the number of women launching businesses in high technology sectors which have greater potential for growth and sustainability is increasing. Accordingly, in Chapter 8, high technology venturing is discussed. It is noted, that the ideas, concept, statistics presented in this book are indicative of those of female entrepreneurs operating in the United Kingdom, Europe and North America. Furthermore, the author is fully aware that such accounts are not fully representative of women in emerging or ethnic communities. Consequently, in an attempt to address this, Chapter 9 looks at the role of entrepreneurship in empowering Palestine women. Finally, the book concludes in Chapter 10 with future research agendas by identifying exciting new research areas.

Chapter 2

The socio-economic context of female entrepreneurship

2.1 INTRODUCTION

This chapter begins by exploring the socio-economic context for female entrepreneurship within regional, national and international economies. Women's experiences of entrepreneurship reflect their position in society; so in order to understand the former it is necessary to explore the latter. An examination of women's position in the labour market and indeed society at large will provide an understanding of the socialisation processes that inform women's decision making when it comes to new venture creation. Given the assumed autonomy associated with independent business venturing, entrepreneurship has been perceived as a particular field that offers women greater agency to control their socio-economic context and so, potentially enhancing their status and power. However, theories of individualisation that over-emphasise freedom and agency have been criticised as they fail to take into account the structural barriers which may influence women's life choices, including those related to their entrepreneurial careers. Consequently, this chapter investigates the structural and contextual barriers that may prevent women from using their agency to build successful and sustainable businesses.

2.2 LEARNING OBJECTIVES

On completion of this chapter, students should be able to:

1   Describe and critique the socio-economic context underpinning female entrepreneurship in most Western developed economies.
2   Clearly articulate and evaluate the influence of the labour market structure on female entrepreneurial activity.
3   Outline and analyse the importance of policy initiatives in encouraging female entrepreneurship.

2.3 LABOUR MARKET STRUCTURE

Since the Second World War, there has been a significant increase in women's involvement in the labour market (Adler and Izraeli, 1988, 1994). This involvement is approximately 45 per cent amongst OECD countries as compared to 30 per cent in countries in, for example, South Asia, the Middle East and North Africa (World Bank, 2006). However, women's increased participation in the labour market has not resulted in gender equality; in part this is due to their feminised labour market participation which is discontinuous, often part-time and/or over-concentrated in poorly paying sectors due to family responsibilities (Warren et al., 2001). Consequently, female labour participation takes an 'M' shape configuration, reflecting discontinuous employment; with women often leaving the labour market between the childbearing years (25–44 years) and returning to employment, typically on a part-time basis as their children grow older (Macran et al., 1996). However, more women returning to work after the birth of their children has resulted in the shrinking of the dip of the 'M'. Although, there has been a decrease in the number of women leaving the labour market to have children, thus resulting in women's labour market participation beginning to reflect a more masculinised pattern of labour market participation, gender equality is not a given (Warren et al., 2001). In fact, despite equal opportunities legislation being inscribed constitutionally in most countries, there may still be instances of gender inequality, the glass ceiling effect, the devaluing of feminine work and family–work conflict (Charles, 2003).

2.4 OCCUPATIONAL SEGREGATION

Occupational segregation is the term used to explain the unequal distribution of men and women across occupations (Charles, 2003). The traditional axes of occupational sex segregation are horizontal and vertical occupational sex segregation. The basis of horizontal segregation is the type casting of occupations as either men's work or women's work (Benschop et al., 2001; Monaghan, 2002). This gendered division of labour is referred to as 'gender typical employment' (Charles, 2003: 267). In fact, it is rare to find an occupation(s) which has equal numbers of men and women engaged or employed (Bielby and Baron, 1984). For example, women's work is stereotypically associated with what Carter and Shaw (2006: 43) refer to as the 'five Cs – caring, cashiering, catering, cleaning and clerical'. Of significant importance is the devaluing of such occupations and their relegation to secondary status in relation to male type jobs which is often reflected in lower remuneration (Armstrong et al., 2003; Charles and Grusky, 2004). In fact, male occupations not only offer greater opportunities for career advancement than female gendered occupations (Hultin, 2003) but, some male gendered jobs even offer a natural progression into self-employment (Holmes, 2007). This is fuelled by apprenticeships in masculine skilled trades such as plumbing and building which have a direct route into self-employment (Carter and Shaw, 2006). However, there is evidence to support the increased entry of women into the 'self-employment route' such as law, accountancy, medicine and veterinary science professions (Marlow and Carter, 2004). Female dominated jobs reflect the role of women as carers and nurturers, and include occupations such as nursing, hairdressing, social work and primary early years teaching; all of which are often referred to as women's work (Williams, 1992). This is the result of gender essentialist ideologies which refer to women as better at and more instinctive carers and nurturers than men (Epstein, 1999; Gerson, 2002). There are of course occasions when individuals cross the gender divide; women in traditional masculine industries has dominated the attention of researchers (Marlow and McAdam, 2011); however, interest in men who cross over into feminine 'type' industries is increasing (Williams, 1992; Cross and Bagilhole, 2002).

Vertical segregation refers to instances whereby men and women occupy jobs within the same occupational sector but due to the deeply cultural embedded ideology of male primacy, men dominate the higher status positions (Bourdieu, 2001; Grusky and Charles, 2001). Simply put, men are pilots, women are air hostesses; men are managers, women are secretaries. The scarcity of women within senior managerial positions is well documented (Oakley, 2000). So, within this era of liberalism, which promotes equality for all, the promise of independent venturing may be seen as a solution to escaping such segregation and in some way may account for the relatively younger age of women business owners (Curran and Blackburn, 2000; Arenius and Kovalainen, 2006). However, if women are leaving the sector early in their careers and/or vertically segregated into lower positions this will make it more difficult for them to accrue the necessary levels of entrepreneurial capital to found and launch successful new start-ups (Boden and Nucci, 2000; Helibrunn, 2004). Occupational segregation thus constrains the accrual of human (education and experience), social (contacts and networks) and symbolic (reputation and credibility) capital necessary to support sustainable businesses (Brindley, 2005; Rouse and Kitching, 2006). Furthermore, occupational segregation (vertical and horizontal) has implications regarding how wealth is distributed and has resulted in a pay gap (Hakim, 1996b; Kelan, 2009). Although most formal barriers have been eliminated resulting in women being able to access the required human and social capital to enable them to obtain higher status jobs, deeply embedded gender ideologies such as essentialist gender stereotypes ensures that sex segregation is still present in modern economies (Charles, 2003).

2.5 GENDER PAY GAP

Although women have improved their educational levels and attainments, this does not necessarily translate into higher earning potential. In fact, Rake *et al.*

(2000) estimated that over his lifespan, a man can expect to earn 37 per cent more than a woman (with no children) with similar educational qualifications. According to the World Economic Forum's Gender Gap Report 'no country in the world has yet managed to eliminate the gender gap' (Hausmann *et al.*, 2006: 3). Some of this divergence can be explained by fewer hours spent by women in the labour market and their greater engagement with part-time work (Carter and Shaw, 2006). Such inequalities continue despite both legal and societal changes. So, for example, the Equal Pay Act is legally inscribed in the statue books of most developed countries and it is now socially accepted that women are an important component of the labour market (Holmes, 2007). However, as noted by Hersch (2006: 352) 'women earn less than men, and no matter how extensively regressions control for market characteristics, working conditions, individual characteristics, children, housework time and observed productivity, an unexplained gender pay gap remains for all but the most inexperienced of workers'.

The ongoing gap between men's and women's earning potential limits the financial rewards available to women (Holmes, 2007). This in turn will have a detrimental effect on the rate of female entrepreneurship as it will restrict the financial resources available to launch and support female enterprises (Carter and Shaw, 2006). Furthermore, it is widely accepted that initial undercapitalisation may have an impact on growth and subsequent performance (Carter and Allen, 1997; Coleman, 2007). Consequently, the persistence of a gender pay gap constrains women's opportunities to amass personal funds for investment purposes (Marlow *et al.*, 2008; Women and Equality Unit, 2008). To sum up, the gender pay gap may influence not only the rate of engagement with entrepreneurial activity but also constrain the contribution of such enterprises to economies worldwide.

2.6 WORK–LIFE BALANCE

Even though there has been significant increase in women's labour market participation, their family responsibilities and age of their children still shapes and informs the type and rate of such activity (Aldrich and Cliff, 2003). Indeed, parenthood still has a greater impact on the working patterns of women whether in paid employment or self-employment than of those of men (Carter and Shaw, 2006). As such, women though holding full-time positions, still assume responsibility for the bulk of household chores, thus limiting the time available for considering, founding and launching a new venture (Aldrich and Cliff, 2003). Although family as an institution can be seen in differing lights, everything from a constraint to an enabler or inspiration, one thing is agreed, in the majority of countries worldwide, household and family responsibilities are seen to be the responsibility of the women folk (Ahl, 2004; de Bruin *et al.*, 2007). As a consequence, it is widely accepted that women work a second shift (Hochschild, 1990); the name given to the double burden that is bestowed on women who work full-time outside the home. As Bradley *et al.* (2000: 84) note 'perhaps the most crucial factor contributing to women's labour market marginalisation is their continued responsibility for domestic work and childcare'.

Within the prevailing entrepreneurial discourse 'patterns of female entrepreneurship are represented in a social space lying at the intersection between the reproductive lifecycle (childlessness, child-bearing, the empty nest, extended motherhood) and the entrepreneurial project' (Bruni *et al.*, 2005: 262). Therefore, women's family and domestic responsibilities may take precedence over their entrepreneurial activity, thus raising doubts over their entrepreneurial credibility and commitment (Galloway *et al.*, 2002; Rouse and Kitching, 2006). Work–life balance challenges will have an impact on women's ability to engage with entrepreneurial activity and as a consequence women's work patterns will not reflect those of their male counterparts (Marlow, 2002). This is particularly evident in the media whereby the female entrepreneur is described in relation to the family business or her role in the family (i.e. coming from a family of entrepreneurs or mumpreneurs). Moreover, the desire to combine work and family commitments results in a high proportion of women-owned businesses operating from within the home (Carter and Shaw, 2006). In the United Kingdom for example, 50 per cent of self-employed women work part-time and over 33 per cent operate their ventures from home (Small Business Service, 2003). In addition their businesses are more likely to contribute a second income to the household (Carter and Shaw, 2006). Although this may be considered a rational and economic response to balancing family and work priorities, such businesses may struggle with projecting legitimacy particularly when it comes to raising Venture Capital and attracting customers (Mirchandani, 1999; Rouse and Kitching, 2006).

The desire for a flexible work schedule is often cited as one of the reasons why women abandon corporate careers to launch a venture of their own (Heliman and Chen, 2003). Thus, entrepreneurship has been cited as one way in which women can balance family and work demands. This is despite evidence suggesting that self-employment provides a poor solution to such competing demands (Greer and Greene, 2003; Williams, 2004). Indeed, self-employed individuals often work longer hours than their paid counterparts (Belle and La Valle, 2003; Blanchflower and Shadforth, 2007). Therefore, the combining of childcare responsibilities with business ownership is not unproblematic (Belle and La Valle, 2003; Rouse and Kitching, 2006).

2.7 WORKPLACE DISCRIMINATION AND THE GLASS CEILING EFFECT

Gender discrimination is defined as 'all processes that lead to a different and often usually disadvantaging behaviour in relation to a person because of his or her gender' (Kelan, 2009: 198). It can be formal, such as legislation forbidding the recruiting of women within certain disciplines, or it may be informal, such as sexual harassment, bullying or hostility from fellow male workers (Williams, 1992). Kanter's (1977) theory of discrimination is based on the power of numbers. Thus, when women represent a small minority within a masculine domain, this can result in tokenism whereby a woman is seen as a representation of her sex as opposed to an individual (Ahl, 2004). Furthermore, due to their minority status, women may encounter exclusionary practices whereby men 'close ranks' including access to networks which may serve to obstruct their progression to senior positions (Hultin, 2003). This may also result in an 'in-group-out-group' mentality during the recruitment process, whereby the dominant group, the in-group, may prevent entry by the out-group and recruit individuals that they consider similar to themselves (Kanter, 1977). This is referred to as homophily or the 'similar to me' effect (Rand and Wexley, 1975). Interestingly, men in female dominated industries are subject to the 'glass escalator effect', whereby men are forced via visible pressures to move out of the female dominated areas and up to those regarded as more appropriate for men (Williams, 1993, 2004). So, discrimination can work to enhance men's position in female dominated sectors where their gender is constructed as positive (Williams, 1992; 2004). However, it appears that only white men are able to benefit from the glass escalator effect (Wingfield, 2009).

It is widely acknowledged that gender discrimination is still a feature of contemporary working life (Kelan, 2010); moreover gender equality does not appear to be on the distant horizon (Charles and Grusky, 2004). However, workplaces and organisations are more often than not constructed as gender neutral (Kelan, 2009). This in effect, presents a backdrop of neutrality where socially characterised prejudices are refuted but given the prevalence and persistence of such discrimination, an ideological dilemma arises (Kelan, 2010). This dilemma requires those whose subject position is bounded by discrimination to deny the institutional basis for such, even when it is clearly evident. Meritocracy within the neoliberal era is seen as the solution to gender equality (Krefting, 2009); whereby the advancement of an individual is based on objective criteria (education, experience and skills) and open to all regardless of gender (Broadbridge and Simpson, 2011). Although women identify situations of discrimination within the workplace (such as fraternity and old boys' network) as a result of meritocracy, they are reluctant to identify such situations as gender disadvantage, instead choosing to rationalise them through individual choice (Kelan, 2009; McRobbie, 2009).

The glass ceiling effect is another form of discrimination and is often cited as a motivating factor for women entering self-employment (Patterson and Mavin, 2009). According to Morrison *et al.* (1987: 13) the glass ceiling is a 'transparent barrier that [keeps] women from rising above a certain level in corporations'. Thus, it is the metaphor applied to the invisible barriers encountered by suitably qualified women as a group trying to progress and advance within their chosen occupations as opposed to their lack of ability to undertake senior positions (Gupta *et. al.*, 2008, 2009). In addition, the glass ceiling barrier which restricts the vertical mobility of women (Baxter and Wright, 2000) is considered to take full effect below the general manager level (Powell and Butterfield, 1994). Simply put, as women progress up the corporate ladder the barriers they encounter intensify relative to those faced by their male counterparts (Hymowitz and Schellhardt, 1986; Baxter and Wright, 2000). Accordingly, enterprise is often seen as an alternative for women who are seeking self-achievement and self-fulfilment (Moore and Buttner, 1997). However, the removal or overcoming of such restrictions may not necessarily result in gender equality due to horizontal occupational segregation (Holmes, 2007). In fact, there has been little change in the gender balance within senior roles since 2008, despite increasing numbers of women graduating with university qualifications and holding middle management positions. Worryingly, according to Turner (2010) the United Kingdom is approximately sixty years away from equal numbers of men and women at the board level and equal pay (Smyth, 2010). A similar situation exists in the United States, where in 2005 only 16.4 per cent of top management positions were held by women (Catalyst, 2006).

2.8 AN ALTERNATIVE PERSPECTIVE – PREFERENCE THEORY

Preference theory acknowledges the relative importance of childbearing on women's lives, including their career choices, and 'emphasises personal values and decision-making at the micro-level' (Hakim, 2003: 350). The contraceptive revolution that took place in the 1960s (in most countries in Western Europe and the United States[1]), and which resulted in the transfer of control of reproduction from men to women, is the starting point for preference theory. As a consequence, the contraceptive revolution, combined with the equal opportunities revolution, resulted in a new scenario for women whereby they had control over their lives, including lifestyle choices that were not previously available to them (Hakim, 2000).

Preference theory acknowledges the heterogeneity amongst women as a group with Hakim referring to a threefold typology of women's work preferences as opposed to a one-size-fits-all approach (Hakim, 1991; 1996a). These three lifestyle preferences determine women's employment patterns and behaviour (Hakim, 2003).

According to Table 2.1, *adaptive* women represent the majority of women and are those women who wish to combine both family and work life. Adaptive strategies include the selection of part-time work or seasonal jobs which provide flexibility. For example, some occupations like teaching are more attractive as this

Table 2.1 *Preference theory: three lifestyle preferences*

Home-centred	Adaptive	Work-centred
20% of women varies 10%–30%	*60% of women varies 40%–80%*	*20% of women varies 10%–30%*
Family life and children are the main priorities throughout life. Equivalent activities in the public arena: politics, sport, art, etc.	This group is most diverse and includes women who want to combine work and family, plus drifters and unplanned careers.	Childless women are concentrated here. Main priority in life is employment.
Prefer *not* to work.	Want to work, but *not* totally committed to work career.	Committed to work or equivalent activities.
Qualifications obtained as cultural capital.	Qualifications obtained with the intention of working.	Large investment in qualifications/training for employment or other activities.
Number of children is affected by government social policy, family wealth, etc.	This group is *very responsive* to: ■ government social policy ■ employment policy ■ equal opportunities policy/propaganda ■ economic cycle/recession/growth, etc.	Responsive to: ■ economic opportunity ■ political opportunity ■ artistic opportunity etc. Not responsive to social/family policy.
Not responsive to employment policy.	Such as: ■ income tax and social welfare benefits ■ educational policies ■ school timetables ■ childcare services ■ public attitude towards working women ■ legislation promoting female employment ■ trade union attitudes to working women ■ availability of part-time work and similar work flexibility ■ economic growth and prosperity, and institutional factors generally.	

Source: Hakim, *Work-Lifestyle Choices in the 21st Century*, Oxford University Press (2000).

allows for the combining of both responsibilities. *Work-centred* women are still in the minority despite the increasing numbers of women gaining educational qualifications. Women within this group may remain childless even if married – with education seen as an investment. The majority of men are work-centred and according to Hakim (2003) the fact that men outnumber women in this group will result in their dominance in the labour market.[2] *Home-centred* women are also a minority (especially in Western societies) and women within this group prioritise family over market work, with the majority remaining at home after they marry. Interestingly education is seen as way to meet potential husbands and to increase their attractiveness to potential spouses. Obviously these preferences are made within different individual, social and cultural contexts and so, resulting in non-uniform outcomes (Hakim, 2003).

2.9 SEGREGATED EMPLOYMENT PATTERNS AND FEMALE ENTREPRENEURSHIP

Given the well-documented occupational segregation and gender inequalities encountered by women, it not surprising that new venture creation has been referred to as one way in which women can escape the constraints of the labour market. Labour market experiences are significant as those entering self-employment usually do so from prior employment where they accumulate many of the resources necessary to commence a new venture (Welter, 2004; Gupta *et al.*, 2009). So, although women business owners constitute a much smaller sub-set of the entrepreneurial population than that of employees, they experience similar disadvantages associated with vertical and horizontal occupational segregation (Marlow, 2002). In fact, women's sectoral concentration when it comes to entrepreneurial activity mirrors their position within the broader labour market where they are horizontally segregated into work designated as lower status and skill and which, in turn, commands lower returns (Halford and Leonard, 2005). As such, occupational divisions and subordination are reproduced as opposed to being challenged with business ownership resulting in women occupying the lower echelons of the retail and service sector (Bruni *et al.*, 2004a), often referred to as the 'pink ghettos' (Fine, 2010: 56).

Accordingly, most female self-employment is confined to traditionally feminised activities such as education, health, catering, caring, personal and business services (Hundley, 2000, 2001a; Carter and Shaw, 2006). However, given ease of access, such sectors are more crowded and competition is stronger with associated implications for profit generation and sustainability (Meager *et al.*, 2003; Roper and Scott, 2007). In effect, the negative impacts of female occupational segregation follow women into self-employment but rather than poorer pay and prospects, the outcome is lower incomes, poorer performance and firm viability (Verheul and Thurik, 2001). Consequently, women are more likely to lack the capital, contacts and experience required to set up in higher performing sectors such as high technology (Turk and Shelton, 2004). So, rather than being an act of freedom and agency, self-employment may be one of constraints (Adkins, 2002). In fact, when it comes to choosing which industrial sector to enter, rather than belonging to the individual, choice is determined by gendered expectations (Ahl, 2004).

Hence, socio-economic positioning influences the industrial sector women chose to enter, as well as the accrual of resources from which they can draw (Marlow, 2002). Therefore, the industrial sectors in which women-owned businesses are predominantly located mirror those which have high levels of female employment (Carter et al., 2001). So, self-employment often reproduces the segregation experienced by women in the labour market and then feeds the cycle of disadvantage (Carter and Shaw, 2006). In fact, Marlow, warns 'if women are looking to self-employment as an escape from pressures and prejudice associated with their gender, business ownership is unlikely to offer a satisfactory solution' (Marlow, 1997: 203).

Contextual, historical and political factors also affect how gender is produced and reproduced (Fenstermaker and West, 2002). In fact, the institutional environment which is country specific can influence gender role patterns, access to markets and thus entrepreneurial activity (Wilson, 2002; Bates et al., 2007). The institutionalised social norms associated with gendered role expectations influence the repertoire of options, choices or opportunities available to individuals (Wilson, 2002; Welter and Smallbone, 2008). Consequently, institutional constraints such as childcare facilities or social and tax policies may play an overt restricting role when it comes to female entrepreneurship (Welter, 2004). It would be an oversight to view women's engagement with entrepreneurial activity solely in terms of market opportunities; instead it is necessary to take into account the societal values attributed to female employment (Polanyi, 1957; Welter, 2004, 2011). Societal norms such as women's role as homemakers and mothers may impact the likelihood of entrepreneurship being considered as a viable career option. In fact, Welter (2004) goes on to argue that women take into account that which is correct and suitable for their gender when making career choices. So, institutional constraints 'in the form of local traditions and norms that determine gender roles within families help explain why female entrepreneurs start in specific, oftentimes low growth and low-income industries' (Welter, 2011: 168).

2.10 POLICIES TO ENCOURAGE FEMALE ENTREPRENEURSHIP

Due to women's potential to contribute to aggregate economic activity, women have been the focus of regional, national and international economic development agencies; with women considered to be an untapped pool of entrepreneurial potential and talent (Marlow et al., 2008). So, in order to tap into this pool and unleash their potential, a number of polices have been implemented aimed at removing barriers preventing women from realising their potential as business owners (Marlow and Carter, 2004). In the United States, such encouragement can be

BOX 2.1 SPOTLIGHT ON SUPPORT INITIATIVES: WOMEN ENTREPRENEUR AMBASSADORS IN SWEDEN

The Government Ambassador Programme was initiated in 2006 by the Swedish government to enable the growth and development of women's entrepreneurship. Recognising that the majority of people in Sweden associate entrepreneurship with men and the fact that only 25 per cent of all businesses are run by women, the Swedish Agency for Economic and Regional Growth identified more than 800 women entrepreneurs to serve as 'ambassadors' to bring greater visibility to women entrepreneurs.

The ambassadors share stories and lessons from their experience in schools, online, at conferences and with various organisations and associations. A key emphasis lies in representing a range of entrepreneurs (age, background, industry, experience) within these corps, to help women better identity themselves with these ambassadors. The ambassadors also blog about issues of importance to them. In addition, they cultivate contacts among Swedish women entrepreneurs, strengthening bonds and ensuring mutual support within this network.

Written by Ulrika Stuart Hamilton, GEM Sweden

Source: GEM 2010 Report: Women Entrepreneurs Worldwide (p. 14).

traced back to 1979 when the US Small Business Administration (SBA) established the Office for Women's Ownership. The establishment of this office demonstrated governmental commitment to supporting female enterprise and it is therefore not surprising that the United States has the highest participation rate of female entrepreneurship amongst all developed economies of 30 per cent. As a result, the United States is often regarded as an exemplar when it comes to female entrepreneurship and the benchmark against which to measure female entrepreneurship in other countries (Marlow *et al.*, 2008). An example of this comes from the United Kingdom where the Department of Trade and Industry states its aim as 'to increase significantly the numbers of women starting and growing businesses in the UK, to proportionately match or exceed the level achieved in the USA' (Small Business Service, 2003: 4). Although the United Kingdom has witnessed the introduction and embedding of a number of initiatives to support female enterprises in the last ten years, such initiatives do not appear to have the longevity of their US counterparts (Carter and Shaw, 2006) and as a result have not delivered to the same degree. In fact, there appears to be a high level of churn within the sector and as a consequence within the United Kingdom, women's

BOX 2.2 SPOTLIGHT ON SUPPORT INITIATIVES: GOING FOR GROWTH IN THE REPUBLIC OF IRELAND

The Going for Growth initiative in Ireland started in 2008 with the aim to inspire women entrepreneurs to pursue growth for their businesses and to provide support for these efforts. It is funded by the European Social Fund, Enterprise Ireland and the Department of Justice and Equality. It is open to 50 per cent or more of Irish companies, and is focused on growth.

Women business owners participate in monthly roundtables led by Lead Entrepreneurs: women who have built and grown successful businesses. The volunteers meet in different locations around Ireland with small groups of women owner-managers to provide advice and support in the development of their businesses. The roundtables are practice-oriented, providing participants with lessons on what has worked and what hasn't worked in real-life situations. The Lead Entrepreneurs share their experiences and facilitate discussion among participants facing common challenges.

Over 150 women entrepreneurs have benefited from participation in previous cycles of Going for Growth. They report that the roundtable sessions led them to make practical changes in their businesses, and helped them achieve their growth goals. Enterprise Ireland is also supporting a follow-on initiative, Continuing the Momentum, for selected participants which have completed a cycle of Going for Growth and continue to be focused in achieving growth. The programme was included among the 2009 EU Good Practices, and voted into the Top 10 of these initiatives. It was also selected to represent Ireland at the 2011 European Enterprise Awards.

Source: Paula Fitzsimons, GEM 2010 Report:
Women Entrepreneurs Worldwide (p. 16).

overall share of the sector has changed very little since 1992 (Marlow *et al.*, 2008). Policy initiatives aimed at increasing female entrepreneurship must just not focus on promoting entrepreneurship as a viable career option or creating an enterprise culture, rather they must take into account the socio-economic context of the countries in which they are implemented, otherwise their impact will be limited (Marlow *et al.*, 2008). Obviously international comparisons do provide some critical insights with regards best practice; however, caution must be exercised as the basis for the data may not be compatible or theoretically/statistically robust.

BOX 2.3 SPOTLIGHT ON SUPPORT INITIATIVES: CULTIVATING WOMEN ENTREPRENEURS IN TAIWAN

The Female Entrepreneur Cultivation Network Plan is one of the programmes initiated under the Female Entrepreneurship Guidance Plan by the Taiwan government's Small and Medium Enterprise Administration. The programme, launched in 2007, is specifically designed to provide a comprehensive range of resources and business connections for female entrepreneurs in cultural and creative industries, the high technology sector, health and beauty, and software. By promoting the dissemination of entrepreneurship experience and knowledge, this initiative aims to encourage female entrepreneurs to focus on innovative, knowledge-intensive fields.

Activities include training courses and consulting services specifically designed for women, grants for research on female entrepreneurship, and networking opportunities for sharing experiences, providing business advice, and offering support and encouragement across multiple cities in Taiwan. In addition, women entrepreneurs with high-growth-potential businesses can participate in award programmes and apply for government subsidies. Women business owners also receive sponsorship to attend international entrepreneurship events, to help them keep pace with international trends.

During the first three years of this programme, over 7,000 women start-up managers have been cultivated and 611 female-owned businesses have been successfully established.

Source: Ru-Mei Hsieh, GEM 2010 Report: Women Entrepreneurs Worldwide (p. 52).

2.11 SUMMARY

The aim of this chapter was to demonstrate how socio-economic positioning results in the gendering of the labour market and subsequently the gendering of self-employment. Thus, it is not surprising that gender segregation within the labour market by type of sector and industry has resulted in a segregated pattern of entrepreneurship by gender with the majority of women-owned businesses within the service sector, where capital requirements are lower and previous work experience irrelevant. So, female segregated employment patterns follow women into business ownership. Furthermore, women's experience of female entrepreneurship appears to be of a similar nature regardless of geographical context.

Given the assumed autonomy associated with independent business venturing, it is often assumed that entrepreneurship offers women greater socio-economic agency and thus, greater scope to enhance their status and power. Moreover, within some forums, entrepreneurship has been held up as a panacea to challenge the subordination of women via the promise of autonomy and independence. In fact, it has been heralded as the saviour for different categories of women including immigrant women, rural women, older women and those women on the poverty line. However, it is important to note that such subordination is deeply embedded within a historical socio-economic context which informs and reproduces normative hierarchies and patriarchies which are unlikely to be addressed by new venture creation alone.

2.12 DISCUSSION POINTS

- The promise of entrepreneurship: is entrepreneurship the solution to some of the challenges faced by women in the labour market such as discrimination? Explain and justify your answer.
- Discuss the relevance of Preference Theory in today's society in explaining entrepreneurial intentions amongst women.
- Critically reflect upon what more can be done by governments worldwide to encourage female entrepreneurship.

Chapter 3

Entrepreneurship as gendered

3.1 INTRODUCTION

The defining masculinity of the entrepreneurial discourse has been recognised for some time; with the embedded message being, 'think entrepreneur, think male'. Evidently, women do not easily 'fit' into the accepted model of entrepreneurship as that which is associated with the feminine is in opposition to normative entrepreneurial action and characterisation. Therefore, this chapter explores the invisibility of women within the entrepreneurial discourse and the attempts made to challenge the so-called 'gender neutrality' of the domain.

3.2 LEARNING OBJECTIVES

On completion of this chapter, students should be able to:

1 Critically analyse the influence of gendered stereotypes upon entrepreneurial intentions.
2 Understand the implications of the androcentric entrepreneurial mentality on female entrepreneurship.
3 Critically evaluate the assumptions underlying the so-called female underperformance hypotheses.

3.3 THE QUESTION SHOULD NOT BE 'WHO IS AN ENTREPRENEUR?' BUT RATHER 'WHO IS AN ENTREPRENEUSE?'

The term entrepreneur originates from the French word entreprendre which translates as 'to undertake' or 'go between' and can be traced back to Cantillon (1755), an Irish economist living in France who introduced the idea that the entrepreneur plays a highly specialised role. As a discursive practice, entrepreneurship produces its own subject; entrepreneur and not entrepreneuse. As a consequence, entrepreneurship has traditionally been associated with men and considered as a form of masculinity (Mirchandandi, 1999; Bird and Brush, 2002). Guiso and Rustichini (2011) even go as far as to claim that entrepreneurship requires high levels of testosterone. So, it is of no surprise that theorists present the entrepreneur as a man and one of extraordinary character; a hero, maverick or self-made man (Hanson, 2003). In fact, Bruni *et al.* (2004b: 407) refer to the entrepreneur as 'the conqueror of unexplored territories, the lonely hero – the patriarch'. However, this discourse only serves to create the entrepreneurial archetype of the white male hero (Ogbor, 2000). Furthermore, in the majority of Western societies the hero myth of the male entrepreneur is reinforced by the media (Drakopoulou-Dodd and Anderson, 2007).

So, entrepreneurship is a male gendered construct – it is not neutral (Marlow and Patton, 2005; Lewis, 2006). The gendered nature of the entrepreneurship discourse has resulted in women being made invisible (Ahl, 2004). As such, the female entrepreneur is marginalised and becomes the 'other', a contradiction to the natural order (de Beauvoir, 1988/1949; Butler, 1990) and so, is an interloper in the field. This analysis suggests that women do not easily 'fit' into the accepted model of entrepreneurship.

3.4 BEM'S SEX-ROLE INVENTORY

An enduring critical illustration of how biological categories are stereotypically mapped onto and inform the gender binary is outlined by Bem (1981) in her 'sex-role inventory'. Associated masculine traits include assertiveness, risk taking, leadership, aggression and individualism, while the feminine scale includes affection, sensitivity, tenderness, gentleness, warmth and sympathy (see Table 3.1). Using Bem's categorisations, Ahl (2004) draws our attention to how those characteristics linked to men are seamlessly associated with the entrepreneurial character – the individualistic, competitive opportunity seeking risk taker (see Table 3.2). Accordingly, that which is associated with masculinity is afforded greater respect, legitimacy and authority, whilst that which is associated with femininity is subordinated within this hierarchical binary (Hirdman, 2001; Bowden and Mummery, 2009). In fact, most of the positive words associated with womanhood in Bem's list, such as affectionate, sympathetic, understanding, compassionate, warm, were not present in the discussion of entrepreneurship or used to describe the entrepreneur. According to Ahl (2004: 54) 'it is quite safe to conclude that the language used to describe entrepreneurship is male gendered. Entrepreneurship is thus a male gendered construct, it is not neutral'.

3.5 SOCIETAL GENDERED EXPECTATIONS

Even though entrepreneurship and its assumed autonomy has been offered as a particular field that offers women greater agency to enhance their status and

Table 3.1 Bem's sex-role inventory

Bem's masculinity scale	Bem's femininity scale
Self-reliant	Affectionate
Defends own beliefs	Loyal
Assertive	Feminine
Strong personality	Sympathetic
Forceful	Sensitive to the needs of others
Has leadership abilities	Understanding
Willing to take risks	Compassionate
Makes decisions easily	Eager to soothe hurt feelings
Self-sufficient	Soft spoken
Dominant	Warm
Masculine	Tender
Willing to take a stand	Gentle
Act as a leader	Loves children
Individualistic	Does not use harsh language
Competitive	Flatterable
Ambitious	Shy
Independent	Yielding
Athletic	Cheerful
Analytical	Gullible
Aggressive	Childlike

Source: Ahl, H.J. (2004) *The Scientific Reproduction of Gender Inequality: A Discourse Analysis of Research Texts upon Women's Entrepreneurship*, Copenhagen, CBS Press (p. 56).

power (Beck, 1992; Giddens, 1992), it is negligent to think that the type of business selected by a woman is solely the result of individual preference (Ahl, 2006). According to McRobbie (2009: 49) 'women are currently being disempowered through the key discourses of empowerment they are offered'. Thus, the decisions and choices relating to independent venturing are gendered and influenced by gendered characterisations, in that some fit the stereotype/identity of a woman more so than others (Fine, 2010). Across societies gendered stereotypes depict women to be caretakers and their place to be within the home, whilst men are considered to breadwinners active within the marketplace; so creating a patriarchal mentality whereby men acquire positions of greater importance and status (Dex, 2003). Worryingly, despite women's increased participation in the labour force, this patriarchy continues with women still taking responsibilities for the bulk of domestic and caring responsibilities (Marlow, 2002).

Gendered stereotypes are socially constructed and are the result of a socialisation process (Lippa, 2002) which starts during childhood, before the age of five and is complete by adolescence (Deaux and LaFrance, 1998; Eagly *et al.*, 2000;

Table 3.2 *Masculinity words compared to enterpreneur words*

Bem's masculinity scale	Entrepreneur
Self-reliant	Self-centred, Internal locus of control, Self-efficacious, Mentally free, Able
Defends own beliefs	Strong willed
Assertive	Able to withstand opposition
Strong personality	Resolute, Firm in temper
Forceful	Unusually energetic, Capacity for sustained effort, Active
Has leadership abilities	Skilled at organising, Visionary
Willing to take risks	Seeks difficulty, Optimistic, Daring, Courageous
Makes decisions easily	Decisive in spite of uncertainty
Self-sufficient	Independent, Detached
Dominant	Influential, Seeks power, Wants a private kingdom and a dynasty
Willing to take a stand	Stick to a course
Act as a leader	Leading economic and moral progress, Pilot of industrialism, Manager
Individualistic	Detached
Competitive	Wants to fight and conquer, Wants to prove superiority
Ambitious	Achievement oriented
Independent	Independent, Mentally free
Athletic	
Analytical	Exercising sound judgement, Superior business talent, Fore-sighted, Astute, Perceptive, Intelligent
Aggressive	
Leftovers	Tolerance for ambiguity, Likes to create

Source: Ahl, H.J. (2004) *The Scientific Reproduction of Gender Inequality: A Discourse Analysis of Research Texts upon Women's Entrepreneurship*, Copenhagen, CBS Press (p. 57).

Wilson, 2002). Not only are gender characterisations socially constructed but they are also socially learned (Gupta *et al.*, 2009). So, by the time an individual reaches early adulthood, they have a clear understanding of the characteristics and qualities associated with each sex (West and Zimmerman, 1987). This is articulated nicely within the arena of school subjects, where assumptions resides, that boys do and are good at 'maths and science' whilst girls are more interested and competent in arts and languages (Nosek *et al.*, 2002). Although the notion that women cannot do maths or science has long been contested, science education is still portrayed in such a way that does not attract women in the same numbers as their male counterparts (Fine, 2010). Thus, stereotypes that differentiate masculinity and femininity are deeply embedded within society and cultural norms (Greene *et al.*, 2011).

3.6 GENDER STEREOTYPES AND ENTREPRENEURIAL INTENTIONS

Stereotypical gender expectations which are influenced by the subject positions attributed to men and women through ascribed masculinities and femininities will influence individuals' perceptions of and receptiveness to certain occupations (Cejka and Eagly, 1999). According to Heilman (1983) occupational preferences are shaped by perceived fit between one's sex and stereotypical characterisations associated with that particular job. Moreover, if there is a perceived lack of fit this will result in the individual having a negative evaluation regarding their ability to perform that job, and so increasing the likelihood of their disengagement with this particular occupation. Within the entrepreneurial field evidence of such negative evaluations has been found (Scherer et al., 1990); in addition to women believing that their environment was less supportive and conducive to entrepreneurial activity (Zhao et al., 2005). In a study which looked at the relationship between individual perceptions and entrepreneurial prosperity, Langowitz and Minniti (2007) found that men's perceptions of themselves were more optimistic, which in turn resulted in increased incentives and intentions to start a business.

The influence of gender stereotypes upon men and women's intentions to pursue entrepreneurship is well documented (Heilman, 2001; Nosek et al., 2009). For example, the association between stereotypical femininity and weakness, lack and powerlessness is self reinforcing and enduring across time and space (Holmes, 2007) and may have a negative impact on entrepreneurial activity. Thus, gendered stereotypes within the context of entrepreneurship map socialised behavioural expectations on to the biological categories of male and female whilst subtly producing and reproducing the devaluation of the feminine (Harding, 1986; Knights and Kerfoot, 2004). Gupta et al. (2009) in their study of the relationship between gender stereotypes and entrepreneurial intentions found that identification with masculine characteristics was positively correlated with entrepreneurial intentions. They also found that gender stereotypes in contemporary society strongly influence men's and women's entrepreneurial intentions. So, even when men and women with the same educational attainments are compared, masculine stereotypes associated with entrepreneurship can have an adverse effect on female entrepreneurial attentions due to their lack of affiliation with masculine traits they perceive to be necessary for entrepreneurial activity (Gupta et al., 2008, 2009). Consequently, the way in which gender and entrepreneurship are socially constructed can influence an individual's entrepreneurial intentions as opposed to mere biological sex (Gupta et al., 2009). Hence, gender stereotypes and ascriptions may explain differences in male and female entrepreneurial activity and the type of entrepreneurial activity engaged in (Marlow, 2002).

Gender stereotypes are both descriptive and prescriptive (Heilman and Wallen, 2004), in other words, beliefs regarding the traits that individuals actually possess determine the traits that they should possess (Eagly *et al.*, 2000; Eddleston and Powell, 2008). Moreover, if a woman challenges prescriptive stereotypes this may result in penalties such as dislike and immense negativity (Heilman and Wallen, 2004). Entrepreneurship is still regarded as manly work (Gupta *et al.*, 2009), so for those women who chose to engage in entrepreneurial activity, powerful cultural pressures still demand that they fulfil and demonstrate their femininity through adherence to particular sexualised body images, domestic proficiency and motherhood (McRobbie, 2009). For example, Pini (2005: 82) documents how the few women who became agricultural leaders carved out gendered roles for themselves that entailed both concealing femininity by wearing dark suits and enacting some aspects of conventional masculinity, but at the same time preserved their femininity by asserting a 'nurturing, communicative and empathic' type of leadership. So, to be taken seriously as leaders, Pini (2005) argues that these female agricultural leaders had to create themselves as a third sex. Finally, the lack of female entrepreneurial role models is much lamented as the entrepreneurial image reflects a strongly masculine tone effectively excluding the feminine (Ahl, 2007). This is evident in the media; the majority of role models are men (Bird and Brush, 2002) and women appear to lack visibility (Baker *et al.*, 1997). So for women who enter the masculine domain of entrepreneurship, they lose an effective protection against stereotype threats, a female role model; with stereotype threat defined as 'the real time threat of being judged and treated poorly in settings where a negative stereotype about one's group applied' (Steele *et al.*, 2002: 385).

3.7 THE IMPLICATIONS OF THE ANDROCENTRIC ENTREPRENEURIAL MENTALITY

The masculinity of the entrepreneurship discourse results in the assumption that the masculine standards of business ownership sets the standard of business which is based on objectives of profit maximisation and wealth creation (Eddleston and Powell, 2008). Such standards are so deeply embedded that they are imposed on women-owned businesses without their relevance ever being questioned (Ahl, 2004). The assumption that stereotypical masculinised models of business operation somehow sets the normative standard of what a typical business should look like is particularly problematic. Indeed once this measure is assumed, women-owned firms which do not reflect such norms become labelled as 'underperforming'. Thus, the failure of women to fit in with the male-centred model of business growth may identify problems with representation, thus leading Gilligan (1982: 2) to remark '*the failure of women to fit existing models of human growth, may point to a problem of representation, a limitation in the conception of the human condition, an omission of certain truths about life*' (emphasis added). One such truth is that the majority of businesses whether owned by men or women do not grow to any considerable size. In effect, many male firm owners also fail to meet preferred standards of performance even though they are based upon stereotypical masculine norms. However, it is the businesses that are owned by women which are singled out as poor performers. Thus, the poor performance label sticks to women and due to a small number of male high performing entrepreneurs, those male venturers which do not perform go unnoticed (Ahl, 2004; Marlow and McAdam, 2011). This is articulated nicely by Ahl (2004: 165) who commented, 'somehow all men get to be free riders on their few growth-oriented fellow businessmen'.

Worryingly, failure to fit within such standards may not only result in women-owned ventures identified as lacking but may also have an impact on the women themselves in relation to their confidence and entrepreneurial self-efficacy (Ogbor, 2000). Unfortunately, the message from the prevailing entrepreneurial discourse is that women need to become more like men and strive to fit within these masculine norms (Marlow and McAdam, 2012). A clear illustration of the ongoing adherence of masculine notions of entrepreneurship comes from Manolova et al. (2007: 421) who advise women to be 'more calculative' in order to 'realize their full growth potential'. Thus, women are encouraged to 'masculinise' themselves (Bruni et al., 2004a: 264), which is commonly referred to as the adoption of the honorary man stance (Calás et al., 2009).

3.8 THE FEMALE UNDERPERFORMANCE HYPOTHESES

The female underperformance hypothesis posits 'all else equal, female entrepreneurs tend to be less successful than their male counterparts in terms of conventional economic performance measures' (DuRietz and Henrekson, 2000: 1). However, it is important to note that normative models of business performance within the entrepreneurship field have been derived from studies based exclusively on male samples (Chell and Baines, 1998). This is significant as differences exist in the profile of male- and female-owned businesses in relation to size (Coleman, 2007), managerial style (Carli and Eagly, 2001), industrial sector (Kalleberg and Leicht, 1991), age of the business (Carter et al., 2001) and costs of finance (DuRietz and Henrekson, 2000; Gupta et al., 2009). So, female-owned businesses tend to be smaller in size, less growth-oriented and less profitable when compared to their male counterparts' (Greene et al., 2003).

At least some of the gender differences in business performance may be accounted for by industrial sector as women-owned businesses tend to be concentrated in retail and service sectors (Marlow and McAdam, 2012). Service and retail services are highly competitive with limited opportunities for growth and profitability (Coleman, 2007). Such sectors yield lower returns than sectors such as technology where men-owned businesses dominate (Allen et al., 2007). Thus, systematic differences in the choice of industry or other structural factors, for example, women-owned businesses tend to be underrepresented in manufacturing and construction, less export oriented and disproportionately reliant on a small number of customers, may help explain the observed differences in performance (DuRietz and Henkreson, 2000). According to Mirchandani (1999: 230) there is 'little analysis of how gendered processes may shape the size of firms, or the tendency to focus on certain industries'. Indeed, evidence exists that once size of the business and sectoral distribution are controlled for, women's failure rates are not significantly different from those of male-owned businesses (Kalleberg and Leicht, 1991; Kepler and Shane, 2007). Thus, concerns about the apparent inability of female enterprises to reach the levels of achievement seen in male-owned businesses, with regards to sales turnover and employment, have sparked some debate regarding the scale, causes – and indeed the very existence of – female under-achievement.

The normative masculine model of entrepreneurial behaviour with its associated behaviours, priorities and expectations certainly disadvantage many women who own part-time, home-based ventures located in crowded, low profit parts of the service sector; these firms are unlikely to meet the normative performance measures which prevail (Marlow and McAdam, 2012). However, the fact that such firms do not meet such criteria does not mean they underperform as they may be doing exceedingly well within their particular market segment. Furthermore, the traditional male-centred model may not allow for female managerial styles or motivations (Marlow and Strange, 1994).

The clear conclusion is that performance differences are not a function of skills shortage or lack of competence in managing the business, but are directly attributable to unequal levels of capitalisation and socio-economic positioning. In other words, when female-owned businesses are capitalised in the same way as male-owned businesses few performance differences are found. This argument is supported by a body of work undertaken by Watson (2002) whose analysis comparing inputs and outputs found no performance differences (outputs) between male- and female-owned businesses – when the inputs, in terms of starting capital, hours worked were statistically controlled (DuRietz and Henrekson, 2000; Watson, 2002). To sum up, feminised operating profiles, which divert from normative models, constrain the performance and so, future prospects of the firm (Boden and Nucci, 2000; Marlow and Patton, 2005).

3.9 SUMMARY

In this chapter, it is evident that the dominant discourse in entrepreneurship has resulted in the reproduction of the androcentric entrepreneurial mentality. Rather than being gender neutral, entrepreneurship is gendered as masculine. Whilst there is greater acknowledgement of entrepreneurship as an activity which is gendered, masculinised models of business operation are still considered the natural benchmark for business performance. It is evident that a gendered socio-economic positioning ensures that women's businesses struggle to perform in a manner which echoes the standards associated with 'successful' enterprises and accordingly, they are represented as lacking. More worrying is the impact that this sense of lack can have on the women themselves who may doubt their own entrepreneurial ability as they struggle to fit within these models.

3.10 DISCUSSION POINTS

- ■ Discuss the impact of the 'think entrepreneur – think male' mentality on female students studying entrepreneurship.
- ■ Identify strategies that may result in increased female student engagement with entrepreneurship.
- ■ Discuss the implications of the so-called underperforming female hypothesis on nascent female entrepreneurs.

Chapter 4

Feminist methodological approaches

4.1 INTRODUCTION

As noted in the previous chapter, the clear message embedded within the entrepreneurial discourse is – 'think entrepreneur, think male'. Consequently, doing entrepreneurship is also doing gender. Although there has been some recognition of the impact of gender on women-owned businesses, it is generally accepted that female entrepreneurship research has traditionally suffered from gender blindness. In an attempt to remedy this, this chapter responds to calls for research methodologies which are theoretically sited within a feminist perspective. The chapter commences with a discussion regarding what gender is. The appropriateness of using gender as a lens as opposed to gender as a variable to investigate women's experiences of business venturing is then addressed. The chapter finishes with an exploration of the life story approach, a gender-sensitive approach which is increasingly used in women's entrepreneurship research in order to overcome the inbuilt biases of standard research methodologies.

4.2 LEARNING OBJECTIVES

On completion of this chapter, students should be able to:

1   Reflect and evaluate upon the use of the term 'gender as socially constructed'.
2   Critically evaluate the limitations of 'gender as a variable' approach as a research technique.
3   Describe and critique the main feminist schools of thought.

4.3 WHAT IS GENDER?

Gender as a term was first introduced to distinguish between biological sex and socially constructed sex (Acker, 1992). However, in today's society gender and sex are used interchangeably, thus neglecting the original differentiation between the terms which emerged in the 1970s (Holmes, 2007). Rather than being a category that an individual belongs to or a property of an individual, gender is 'a relationship which brings about redefinitions of subjectivities and subject positions over time, both as products and as producers of social context' (Calás and Smircich, 1996: 241). So, gender refers to socially constructed roles, expectations and patterns which society has devised for each sex and distinctions made between masculine and feminine are socially constructed as opposed to physiological characteristics (Acker, 1992). Furthermore, the appreciation of gender as socially constructed acknowledges that society as opposed to nature determines femininity and masculinity (Holmes, 2007). The notion of gender as socially constructed is thought to have been initiated by the work of Simone de Beauvoir, who famously stated, 'one is not born but rather, becomes a woman' (de Beauvoir, 1988/1949: 295).

Objectifications of gender begin at birth or at ultrasound with what Butler refers to as 'girling the girl', activating gender stereotypes relating to respective sex categories (Butler, 1993: 7–8). Thus, the announcement of either *'It's a girl'* or *'It's a boy'* results in the ascription of descriptive adjectives relating to respective sex categories. Those adjectives contain norms, expectations and specific conations which are internalised (Ahl, 2004) and so men and women serve to re-create the gender system (Hirdman, 1992). Such gendered ascriptions are socially constructed and mapped onto biological sex categories (Harding, 1987; Butler, 1990, 2004). However, whilst it is agreed that there is no essential femininity or masculinity, gender makes us culturally intelligible (Butler, 2004; Holmes, 2007); as social actors we make sense of others in terms of their ascribed gender. Thus, the notion of gendered identities is critical in order to understand the ontology of the constructed subject positions ascribed to men and women through ascribed masculinities and femininities (Bowden and Mummery, 2009).

Gender is neither fixed nor stable, in fact it is constructed through daily interactions with others and as a result individuals learn how to play the part of man or woman depending on what a given context demands or what is considered appropriate (Goffman, 1987). As a result of this gender socialisation process 'we learn what it means to be an adult human being within our society' (Holmes, 2007: 41). In fact, if an individual does not behave appropriately with regards to their gender this may result in them being rejected or sanctioned (West and Zimmerman, 1987). For example, self-promoting men are viewed positively whilst self-promoting women are considered aggressive and thus viewed negatively (Wilson, 2002). Moreover, challenging gender conformity creates 'gender trouble' (Butler, 1993; Jagose, 1996; Roseneil, 2000), as disputing the alleged 'natural order' results in uncertainty and suspicion (Fiske, 1989; Keltner, 1995). For example, such gender trouble is evident in the homophobic reactions towards gay men and women particularly when their biological sex contradicts their assumed gender performances (Fine, 2010).

4.4 IS GENDER A PERFORMANCE OR A PERFORMATIVE?

There is ongoing debate amongst feminist theorists as to whether gender is something which is done 'by' or 'to' (Holmes, 1997). West and Zimmerman (1987) first introduced the concept of 'doing gender', whereby gender is performed as opposed to something people have or possess. Performances can be words or behaviour, for example the phrase 'It's a girl!', rather than being a neutral description of a female identity is a performative statement. According to West and Zimmerman (1987: 125) 'doing gender involves a complex of socially guided perceptual, interactional and micro political activities that cast particular pursuits as expressions of masculine and feminine natures'. Gender performances change depending on the audience and the impression that the individual wants to portray (Nadin, 2007). This results in the fluidity of gender whereby 'each practice of gender is a moving phenomenon done quickly [often] non-reflexively in concert or interactions with others' (Martin, 2003: 352). So, how we perform our gendered roles is complex with degrees of agentic fluidity reflective of the specific context. Such repertoires of gendered practices are available to both men and women such that we adopt elements and degrees of both masculine and feminine behaviours. The fact that people do gender, portrays degrees of agency; however such agency is constrained by societal pressures including gender socialisation and patriarchy (Essers and Benschop, 2007).

According to Butler (1990) it is important to distinguish performance from performativity, with performativity defined 'as the process through which gendered subjects are constituted by regulatory notions within a heterosexual matrix' (Kelan, 2010: 180). According to Butler (1993: 13) 'a performative is that discursive practice that enacts or produces that which it names'. For example, the statement '*I pronounce you man and wife*' at the marriage ceremony, changes the status of the couple. So, rather than being performed, gender is imposed on individuals and does us; leaving little room for personal agency as there is 'no doer behind the deed' (Butler, 1990: 25). Furthermore, there is a ritual dimension to performativity whereby stylised gender acts such as the way we talk and walk are repeated; we make these acts a reality over and over again by performing these actions, thus gender is a constructed masquerade to which we willingly subscribe (Butler, 1990). Holmes (2007) takes the performative notion of gender further and argues that gender is something we do within social constraints, namely interaction with others and it is this interaction with others which determines how we should behave and act in accordance with our gender.

4.5 GENDER BLINDNESS

Although recent years have witnessed an expansion in the extant body of literature regarding women's entrepreneurship (Carter and Shaw, 2006), this has not been matched with appropriate theoretical frameworks, theory building and conceptual analyses such as those regarding feminism and gender (Marlow, 2002; Ahl, 2004, 2006). Indeed, links between existing feminist literatures within the fields of sociology, economics and politics, for example, are rarely utilised to frame explanatory theories to analyse women's experiences of self-employment and business ownership (Mirchandani, 2005). Rather, there has been a propensity to develop atheoretical explorations of women's experiences of self-employment and business ownership rather than embedding such experiences within pertinent conceptual frameworks. In addition, there has been a distinct tendency towards feminist empiricism, (Kepler and Shane, 2007) with early analyses focusing on comparative studies of men and women to ascertain whether gendered assumptions and ascriptions did actually impact upon entrepreneurial activities and experiences (Cromie and Hayes, 1988; Kalleberg and Leicht, 1991; Cromie and Birley, 1992). However, such analyses have only served to reinforce and reproduce the androcentric entrepreneurial mentality (Bruni et al., 2004a).

4.6 FEMINIST EMPIRICISM

The tendency to analyse women's experiences in relation to and in comparison with male entrepreneurs (Mirchandani, 1999; Lewis, 2006; Kepler and Shane, 2007) is referred to as feminist empiricism, or gender as a variable approach. The reliance on feminist empiricism has resulted in the use of conventional cross-sectional survey data where the informant's gender is used as an independent variable in quantitative analysis (Foss, 2010). Furthermore, such standard research methods based on positivist assumptions about reality and methodology either introduce the sex of the entrepreneur as a variable or use samples of male entrepreneurs to research female entrepreneurship (Brush et al., 2009). In effect, this constructs a normative frame which draws upon the masculine as a natural benchmark which has been exacerbated and reinforced by the use of male-gendered measuring instruments (Stevenson, 1990). Feminist empiricism results in the invisibility of women entrepreneurs as their experiences are incorporated into mainstream research (Harding, 1987; Sundin, 1988; Holmquist and Sundin, 1988) and no matter how 'useful and explanatory as these approaches are for men, we cannot be sure they adequately reflect the organising process and organisations of women' (Bird and Brush, 2002: 42). Furthermore, this approach fails to recognise the heterogeneity of women as a group, in addition to the institutional and contextual factors that may impact on our understanding of female entrepreneurship as a research area (Ahl, 2004).

4.7 USING GENDER AS A LENS TO EXPLORE FEMALE ENTREPRENEURSHIP

Researching women's experiences of business ownership has historically been met with methodological challenges (Stevenson, 1990). The overreliance on positivist research methodologies and more recently the ability of such approaches to explain real life phenomena have been questioned (Carter et al., 2007). In fact, according to Hamilton (2006: 256) such approaches, 'commonly reflects and reinforces the relative silence and invisibility of women in entrepreneurial discourse'. Although the concept of gender emerged into mainstream debate in the 1970s (Oakley, 1972) it was not until the 1990s, that studies began to use gender as a lens as opposed to sex to explore entrepreneurial activity. As mentioned earlier, prior to this, biological sex was used in entrepreneurship research to explain the differences in rates of activity between male and female ventures (Gupta et al., 2008). The use of gender as a lens enables the exploration of how gender and entrepreneurship is constructed within society and the impact of such on rates and types of entrepreneurial activity (Gupta et al., 2009). So, the question is no longer focused on whether gender impacts business ownership but how (Marlow, 2002). Such research is invaluable being reflective of, and sensitive to, the influence of gender as a hierarchical system which subordinates the feminine (Ahl, 2004). Moreover, it challenges from where the knowledge base originated and evolved and thus may facilitate the challenging of masculine normative standards (Hurley, 1999).

4.8 FEMINIST RESEARCH METHODOLOGIES[1]

In the section which follows, a brief overview of the main feminist schools of thought is provided. It is important to note that despite being distinct from each other, they all share a common emphasis on the domination of men and consequent subordination of women which is embedded within the fabric of society (Ferguson, 1989; Flax, 1990). Liberalist feminism and social feminism are the two most commonly used feminist perspectives in entrepreneurship research (Ahl, 2004). Liberal feminism focuses on sameness and refers to women becoming more like men as the ideal standard. Social feminism focuses on difference and claims that women bring their own unique and special skills to business and though different to their male counterparts are just as worthy of celebration.

4.8.1 Liberal *feminist* theory

Liberal feminism posits that men and women are essentially similar with regards mental capacities and rationalities and as such are entitled to the same opportunities (Hakim, 2006; Holmes, 2007). Thus, any disadvantage, difference or deprivation experienced by women in relation to men is either due to overt discrimination or structural barriers which restricts their access to essential resources such as education, work experience, mentoring, social networks and funding (Fischer et al., 1993; Greer and Greene, 2003). Consequently, it is sometimes referred to as the 'equality of opportunity perspective' (Neergaard et al., 2011: 5). The absence or abolition of such discriminatory practices would then result in women's achievement equalling that of men; in other words becoming more like men (which is the desired standard) (Ahl, 2004). Liberalist thinking was apparent in the suffrage movement in the United Kingdom and United States during the nineteenth century and is based on ideals of equal rights and opportunities (Holmes, 2007). The approach has been criticised for ignoring the heterogeneity of women by predominately focusing on white middle class women (Alvesson and Due Billing, 1999). According to Beasley, (2005: 34) '(i)f liberal feminism were a shirt it would probably be pinstriped and have shoulder pads. It dresses for success'.

Much of the early research conducted on female entrepreneurship adopted a liberal feminist approach. So for example, when liberalist feminist theory (Fischer *et al.*, 1993) is applied to the so-called underperformance of women-owned businesses, it emerges that such underperformance is the result of discrimination (by lenders) and the lack of human capital (education and industry specific work experience). Furthermore, the liberal feminist view would argue that eliminating stereotypes associated with women's limitations in high technology venturing is the answer to levelling the playing field in this particular industrial sector (Calás *et al.*, 2009). This is nicely articulated by Godwin *et al.* (2006) who argue that women can overcome the gender stereotypes evident within masculine industries if they partner with men and form mixed-sex entrepreneurial teams. Thus, these authors argue that aligning with men would enable women to access resources, opportunities and networks; so increasing their credibility and economic outcomes. As a consequence, any attempt to remove structural barriers such as discrimination associated with stereotypical expectations actually serves to reinforce the stereotype that women 'can't do entrepreneurship' (Ahl, 2006). As to be expected, one of the key criticisms levied against this approach is the alleviation of the male norm as the desired standard and the notion that in order to advance, women must become more like men (Holmes, 2007). Hence, it is the responsibility of women to adapt in order to fit into the present system.

4.8.2 Social feminist theory

In an effort to address the so-called class discrimination of the liberalist feminist approach, social feminist theory which is influenced by Marxist theory acknowledges the impact of class order (Mills and Voerman, 1997). Furthermore, proponents of social feminist theory argue that men and women are essentially different, yet the motivations, beliefs, and characteristics of both men and women are of equal importance. Such differences are considered to be the result of the socialisation processes encountered as result of upbringing whereby boys and girls are taught different skills and values (Ahl, 2004). The approach resulted in the emergence of essentialist terms such as the 'female advantage', 'female Leadership' and 'women's ways'; with feminine traits seen as beneficial and thus to be used constructively (Ashcraft, 2009). Even outside the arena of entrepreneurship, the differences between men and women are conceptualised in popular literature such as *Men are from Mars, Women are from Venus.*[2] When applied to the underperformance of women-owned businesses, social feminist theory claims that such underperformance is due to inherent differences in men and women as a result of differences in early and ongoing socialisation (Fischer *et al.*, 1993). As such, women are not inferior to men but have different traits and skills, which though different to those possessed by men are equally as effective and should be viewed as complementary (Acker, 1992). This approach has been criticised on the grounds of essentialism and polarisation of men and women (Holmes, 2007). Moreover, this approach uses white middle class women as the norm within a North American context ignoring other ethnic, minority or geographical groupings (Ahl, 2004).

4.8.3 Poststructuralist feminist theory

According to Ahl (2004: 35) 'poststructuralist feminist research avoids essentialism and polarizing men and women and sees gender including the body as a socially constructed phenomenon that is culturally historically and locally specific'. Poststructuralist feminism argues that gender is socially constructed through discursive practices and thus it is more appropriate to talk of gender as opposed to sex categories (Weatherall, 2002; Holmes and Meyerhoff, 2003). In other words, language has a role to play in the construction of gendered identities. Consequently, proponents of the approach critically analyse the sexist construction and hegemonic assumptions underpinning narratives, which shape our understanding of activities, such as entrepreneurship (Ahl, 2006). Thus, the task for a poststructuralist feminist organisational scientist is to 'challenge and change the dominant and colonising discourse over and over again' (Calás and Smircich, 1996: 245). Rather than studying female entrepreneurship against scales of sameness (liberal feminism) or difference (social feminism), poststructuralism considers how gender is constructed in different contexts (Ahl, 2004). Furthermore, poststructuralism proposes the idea of not only the fragmented identity but also multiple identities (Ahl, 2004).

4.9 INTERSECTIONALITY OF GENDER

A word of caution has been posited with regards to the consideration of gender in isolation (Allen, 2003) or gender as generic (Ashcraft, 2009, 2011). So for instance, the dynamic manner in which femininity intersects with race, age and class to mould entrepreneurship ensures that there are greater differences within the category of 'the female entrepreneur' per se than there are between male and female business owners (Doyle and Paludi, 1998; Ahl, 2007). This has lead to the concept of intersectionality which acknowledges the interplay between different markers of identity (Ashcraft, 2009). Intersectionality as a term originated from the work of Crenshaw (1997), who criticised mainstream feminist discourse for being white in origin and association. Intersectionality continues to be at the centre of debates looking at power dynamics from the perspective that argues interdependence between intersecting inequalities of gender, race, sexuality, age, disability, social class, religion and nationality, in relation to subject positions and identities (Adib and Guerrier, 2003; Holvino, 2010). Overlapping and intersecting markers of identities are informed by prevailing social stereotypes resulting in narrowing of the characterisations available to our enacted subjectivity (Butler, 1993; Gill and Ganesh, 2007). Accordingly, it is a useful analytical framework as it can aid the illumination of differences, contractions and ambiguities when multiple identities connect to construct the entrepreneurial identity (Crenshaw, 1997; Essers and Benschop, 2009). However, according to Broadbridge and Simpson (2011), it is important that gender is intersected as 'gender with' as opposed to 'gender and', so as not to dilute the focus on gender.

4.10 QUEER THEORY

Queer theory emerged from gay politics and challenges heteronormative assumptions within specific socio-economic contexts as opposed to inequalities (Beasley, 2005). Although queer theory has its origins in gay and lesbian studies, it does not refer solely to gays and lesbians but rather to anything or anyone that departs from what society considers normal (Butler, 1990). There is a dearth of queer analyses upon entrepreneurial activities; as a field of study, entrepreneurship is remarkably conservative and embedded within heteronormativity. Heteronormativity is defined as 'the view that institutionalised heterosexuality constitutes the standard for legitimate and expected social and sexual relations' (Ingraham, 2002: 76). Thus, it is a term describing the marginalisation of non-heterosexual lifestyles and the view that heterosexuality is the normal sexual orientation (Holmes, 2007). There is considerable social, heteronormative pressure to observe gender conformity and convention; 'boys will grow into men who will desire women. Man and woman will then reproduce and all will be as it should be' (Butler, 1993 cited in Holmes, 2007: 83). Queer theory illustrates that the overtly rejecting of ascribed gendered roles is a risky activity; creating 'gender trouble' (Roseneil, 2000: 26) through the rejection of normative ascriptions provokes hostility when these alleged 'natural orders' are disturbed (Keltner, 1995; Whitehead, 2008). Butler (1990) refers to the concept of a drag queen as a good example of 'gender trouble' as it challenges the fictional fixity of gender. Queer theory opposes the exclusionary and regulatory nature of the homo/heterosexual binary in addition to the idea of a 'unified homosexual identity' (Roseneil, 2000: 2). Approaches such as queer theory are invaluable as they challenge heteronormativity which in itself serves to preserve the gender binary (Ashcraft, 2009).

4.11 FEMINIST SENSITIVE APPROACHES – LIFE STORY APPROACH

This section explores gender-sensitive approaches to researching women's entrepreneurship in an attempt to overcome the inbuilt biases of standard research methodologies. Until recently, there has been a predominance of cross-sectional survey techniques in entrepreneurial research, which do not provide 'first hand, real and authentic experiences of entrepreneurial lives' (Foss, 2010: 83). As Haynes (2010) notes, normative methodologies usually favour research instruments which reflect masculine priorities – they search for data upon things or activities which men value or where they excel. This is evident in the case of entrepreneurship where methodological foci concentrate upon issues of risk taking, opportunity searches, growth rates, economic returns and market visibility. Whilst such issues are of interest, they axiomatically narrow the field of investigation to those who fit this 'mould'. However, there is evidence of the increasing use of discourse and life history narrative methods in entrepreneurship research (Hjorth and Steyaert, 2004; Lindh de Montoya, 2004). The use of such methods in the area of female entrepreneurship has been supported by Brush et al. (2009: 16) who argue 'also fruitful could be drawing on some of the less accepted methods of doing research such as content and discourse analysis'. This has been further supported by a growing presence of interpretivist research into entrepreneurial praxis as a concept, notably in Europe but also in the United States (Blackburn and Smallbone, 2008; Gartner, 2010).

Mallon and Cohen (2001) in particular support the use of life history research which allows women to voice their stories and make sense of their experiences in order to better understand their organisational and entrepreneurial realities. According to Reinharz (1992: 126) life history research 'is a feminist encounter because it creates new material about women, validates women's experience, enhances communication among women, discovers women's roots and develops a previously denied sense of continuity'. The use of oral history within female entrepreneurship is premised upon gaining insight into deeper and different understandings of the role of gender upon entrepreneurial intentions and actions. Moreover, the appropriateness of life story narratives is strengthened by their ability to illuminate the intersectionality of gender (Buitelaar, 2007). For the female business owner, this approach is appropriate as it sites experiences of entrepreneurship within the wider context of their lives where no written or other form of record exists thus providing a vehicle through which they can voice their identities (Essers and Benschop, 2009). Life history research can be positioned between ethnography, sociology and history. It offers a distinctive and

39

central voice to the subject and as such, acts as a bridge between personal biographies and the social context upon which the biography is inscribed (Leavy, 2007: 155). Obviously, the accuracy of such accounts may be questioned due to the application of flattering hindsight, however, it is still considered an effective representation of lived experience particularly for women (Eskers and Ben chop, 2009).

4.12 SUMMARY

It is evident from the prevailing discussion in this chapter that doing entrepreneurship is also doing gender. However, although increasing, the use of gender as a lens to explore entrepreneurial activity is still under-utilised. This chapter responds to contemporary calls to embed feminist perspectives within the entrepreneurial field of enquiry by presenting an overview of key political feminist perspectives. It is important to note that even though they all have a different emphasis, they do, however, share a common belief regarding the subordination of women and the subsequent desire to change this ordering. Consequently, it was illustrated that the adoption of gender as a lens is critical in order to demonstrate that the assumed behavioural differences ascribed to men and women arise from ingrained social training, habits, expectations and pressures to conform to contextualised displays of masculinity and femininity. Finally, it was posited that researchers within the field have a role in challenging heternormativity which only serves to restrict discussion beyond the traditional gender binary of man and woman. This role calls for greater reflexive criticism regarding the epistemological assumptions which shape the current research agenda within the female entrepreneurial domain.

4.13 DISCUSSION POINTS

- Discuss the contribution of feminist empiricism to the area of female entrepreneurship. Explain and justify your answer using examples.
- In contrast to feminist empiricism, the researcher will have a prominent role to play in feminist sensitive research. Discuss the implications of this.
- Apart from the life history approach what other approaches could be considered feminist sensitive?

Chapter 5

Family in women-owned businesses and women in family businesses

5.1 INTRODUCTION

This chapter is divided into two sections in order to address the role of family on women's ability and willingness to engage with entrepreneurial activity and the contribution of women to the area of family business. Accordingly, the intersection of the business and family domains are explored. The notion of women as caretakers which is still prevalent in most Western countries within the domestic domain plays an important role in determining the extent to which women engage with the labour market and entrepreneurship. Thus, women's domestic and family obligations and their impact on the rate and type of entrepreneurial activity engaged with, is discussed. Though often challenging to ascertain, women's contribution to family business will also be addressed within this chapter. Within the context of family business, women may be founders, owners, copreneurs, daughter-heirs, or hold various other supporting roles.

5.2 LEARNING OBJECTIVES

On completion of this chapter, students should be able to:

1   Identify and critique the key familial factors underlying women's engagement with entrepreneurial activity.
2   Critically reflect upon the 5M framework.
3   Critically evaluate the contribution of women to the family business domain.

5.3 THE DOUBLE SHIFT

Women's participation in the labour market has increased considerably on a worldwide basis and this has had a significant impact on family life and family composition (Shelton, 2006). For example, within the North American context, there has been a huge increase in the number of women working outside the home resulting in the dual income household (Aldrich and Cliff, 2003). Even though women's participation in paid employment has increased dramatically over the last twenty years, within most Western countries socially constructed expectations exist that burden women with the primary responsibility for domestic labour and childcare (Rouse and Kitching, 2006; Bradley, 2007). According to Bianchi and Casper (2000: 29) 'although US mothers of young children are much more likely to work in the 1990s than they were in the 1970s, which implies an increasing attachment of women to market work, married mothers tend to scale back their hours during their children's preschool years'. Even within the cotemporary era, family responsibilities and age of dependent children still shapes and informs women's engagement with paid employment (Aldrich and Cliff, 2003).

It appears that the increased participation with the labour market does not absolve women from domestic labour and related caring responsibilities; in fact they still retain sole or majority responsibility for such tasks resulting in a double shift or second shift (Hochschild, 1990) giving weight to Mirchandani's (1999) claim that the home is a gendered site. Research conducted on the distribution of household tasks consistently demonstrates that women spend more time on and take more responsibility for domestic duties; with women on average doing 70 per cent of the domestic work within the home (Hochschild, 1990; Baxter, 2000). Interestingly, there has been little decrease in women's contribution despite their increased participation in paid employment with women continuing to carry the burden of domestic work (Baxter, 1997). In fact, according to Ashcraft, (2009: 314) housework is often constructed as 'voluntary acts of care' or 'a labour of love', which only serves to construct activities that are considered maternal as secondary to those associated with market work.

Research on housework has moved away from concentrating on actual proportions completed by men and women to perceptions of its equality and fairness; so despite unequal allocation of domestic work, many women perceive its distribution to be fair (Baxter, 2000). According to Coltrane (2000: 1208) 'on average, women perform two or three times as much housework as men, and the vast majority of men, as well as most women, rate these arrangements as fair'. It appears that women's satisfaction with the division of labour is not based on the equal distribution of tasks or time spent on domestic duties but rather on the nature of the task performed by their male partners (Baxter, 2000). Whilst this gendered division of labour is commonplace in most households (persistent and constituent across countries) (Holmes, 2007), it is noted by Baxter (2000), rather than 50 per cent being considered the point of equity, when it came to the male contribution to household tasks, 34 per cent was considered acceptable with women believing that men were pulling their weight when they were left with 66 per cent of household tasks. Although men do contribute more to domestic duties, women continue to assume responsibility for the bulk of household chores and Young and Willmott's (1973) predication of 'symmetrical family' whereby chores are shared equally amongst the men and women within the household has yet to materialise.

5.4 IMPACT OF FAMILY ON BUSINESS

As a result of specialisation in household production, women are less able to participate in the labour market (Cowling and Taylor, 2001) and for those that do, due to assuming responsibility for the bulk of household chores, have limited time for considering, founding and launching a new venture (Aldrich and Cliff, 2003). However, entrepreneurship has been lauded as a means not only to escape discrimination and glass ceiling effects but also as a vehicle through which women can balance work and family responsibilities (Rouse and Kitching, 2006). In fact, the desire for a flexible work schedule is often cited as one of the reasons why women abandon corporate careers to launch a venture of their own (Heliman and Chen, 2003). Furthermore, women with younger children often view entrepreneurship as a means of balancing the need for flexible working whilst maintaining a professional profile (Caputo and Dolinksky, 1998).

The relationship between domestic responsibilities and work status is an important factor in women's entrepreneurial decisions (Parker, 2009). Accordingly, the operating profiles of female-owned firms also exhibit feminised working patterns; the available data indicates that around half of self-employed women work part-time (less than 30 hours per week) and around a third base their businesses within the home (Danhauser, 1989). Men however, reflect their stereotypical employment profile with much lower rates of part-time and home working, 18 per cent and 24 per cent respectively (Bosma and Harding, 2006; Thompson et al., 2009). Women adopt such operating profiles in an effort to combine economic activity, domestic labour and childcare (Belle and La Valle, 2003; Rouse and Kitching, 2006). Time allocation between household production and entrepreneurial activity contributes to overall performance (Kanazawa, 2005) and women wishing to specialise in the former tend to concentrate in industries where entry barriers and start-up costs are low and in particular whose work schedules accommodate domestic responsibilities (Hundley, 2001a). Therefore, rather than exhibiting agency, women who operate home-based ventures on a part-time basis to fit around domestic duties are responding to the ascribed societal roles of women as nurturers and carers (Holmes 2007). Drawing from an econometric analysis of returns from self-employment, Hundley (2001a: 825) notes unequivocally, 'the presence of small children and greater hours of housework have a negative effect on female earnings'.

Female entrepreneurs often experience a sense of guilt and/or conflict when trying to reconcile their family and work commitments (Duberley and Carrigan,

2012). This is particularly evident amongst those female business owners who have children and as result may experience greater demands on their time and energy which then may detract from the time they can devote to their business in comparison to those without children (Renzulli *et al.*, 2000). Interestingly, Hundley's (2000, 2001a) findings demonstrate that women without children out-perform men in terms of earnings. As such, encouraging more women into entrepreneurship is not a straightforward solution to achieving work–life balance and in fact, evidence suggests that self-employment provides a poor solution to such competing demands; as Weiler and Bernasek (2001) caution that such arrangements may actually burden women further due to reduced salaries and increase family responsibilities.

5.5 MARKET WORK VERSUS HOUSEWORK

It is wrong to assume that 'women act from similar motivations and look for simi-lar rewards from entrepreneurial activity as their male counterparts' (Marlow and Strange, 1994: 173). In fact, many married mothers often perceive self-employment and working from home as a means to facilitate housework (Hilbrecht *et al.*, 2008). So, it appears that closer proximity to children is often a key determinant in women's decision to locate their businesses at home, and as such will be drawn towards industrial sectors with low barriers to entry and start-up costs (Hundley, 2000). However, such proximity also brings with it an increas-ing probability of family responsibilities interfering with work tasks (Hundley, 2001b). In fact, Mirchandani (1999: 232) comments 'many businesses which are small and home-based are owned by women; their female ownership in turn affects the ability of the business to grow and to maintain a separation from the demands of the provision of family care'. Men on the other hand, when faced with the same scenario, are more likely to work outside of the home in an effort to con-centrate solely on their ventures away from family distractions (Hundley, 2001b). However, those men that do locate their businesses at home appear to be more adept at separating their work responsibilities from family impositions (Rowe and Bentley, 1992).

5.6 FAMILY EMBEDDEDNESS

It has been suggested that recent studies on the family embeddedness perspective of entrepreneurship (Aldrich and Cliff, 2003) or 'enterprising households' (Jennings and McDougald, 2007) may hold promising avenues for future research on women's entrepreneurship (de Bruin *et al.*, 2007). In fact, such family units/ systems can act as either an enabler or barrier to entrepreneurial activity. On the one hand, family obligations can detract energy and time from entrepreneurial activities with subsequent impact on growth and performance of the venture, whilst on the other, entrepreneurship can give women more flexible arrangements to balance family and work commitments. In some cases family life can actually be the inspiration for entrepreneurial activity; this is nicely summed up by Brush *et al.* (2009: 7) who commented that family households 'might allow women to detect innovative opportunities arising from household and family contexts'. In addition, the family represents an important resource for new ventures including financial and human resources (Steier and Greenwood, 2000; Chrisman *et al.*, 2002). Bruce (1999) found that having a husband with some exposure to self-employment nearly doubles the probability that a woman will become self-employed. Moreover, Moult and Anderson (2005) refer to 'windows of opportunity' which are presented to mature women as a result of diminishing domestic responsibilities including childcare provision. To conclude this section, although family can be seen in differing lights, everything from constraints to enablers or inspiration, one thing is agreed, it is the woman's responsibility (Ahl, 2006).

5.7 THE '5M' FRAMEWORK

A 'family embeddedness perspective on entrepreneurship implies that researchers need to include family dimensions in their conceptualising and modelling, their sampling and analysing and their interpretations and implications' (Aldrich and Cliff, 2003: 574). This has resulted in the 5M framework which builds on the 3M model which cites 'marketing', 'money' and 'management' as the three basic building blocks for business viability and growth (Bates *et al.*, 2007). The rationale for this extension is based on the assumption that entrepreneurship is a socially embedded phenomenon (Davidsson, 2003; Steyaert and Katz, 2004). This assumption results in the inclusion of 'motherhood' and 'macro/meso environment'. 'Motherhood' represents the household/family context and acknowledges that such a context may have a greater impact on women than their male counterparts (Jennings and McDougald, 2007). The 'macro/meso environment' includes societal expectations and cultural norms (macro) and intermediate structures and institutions (meso) (Aldrich, 1989) and more importantly the limitations they may impose on the options available to female entrepreneurs. So, social, cultural and institutional norms not only affect the recognition and enactment of opportunities by female entrepreneurs but also theirs and others' perceptions of their ventures. Consequently, the 5M model expands the frame through which entrepreneurial endeavours are analysed and 'makes explicit the social embeddedness of women entrepreneurs by reflecting the multiple levels of influence on their entrepreneurial actions' (Brush *et al.*, 2009: 8). Finally, the framework acknowledges the interaction between the accrual and use of entrepreneurial

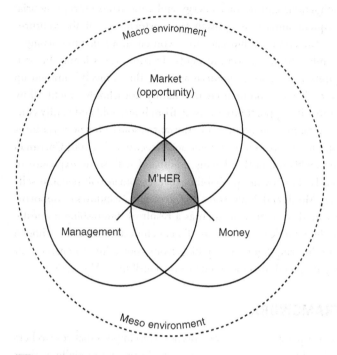

Figure 5.1
The 5M framework

Source: Brush *et al.*, 2009: 8.

capital (the focus of the next chapter) and the influence of the domestic and institutional context (see Figure 5.1).

5.8 FAMILY BUSINESS

Historically, women have been supporting family businesses for centuries (Pepelasis Minoglou, 2007) and may be founders, owners, copreneurs, daughter-heirs (Hollander and Bukowitz, 1990; Poza and Messer, 2001). Baines and Wheelock (1999: 1) in a study identified some common characteristics of family businesses such as 'long hours, the use of the family home as a workplace, a stereotypical gender division of labour and cooperative, reciprocal values operating at the level of the household'. Traditionally women have operated as the care-takers and nurturers within the home environment which has resulted in an assumption regarding the unpaid contributions of women not only as domestic labourers but also as invisible, unpaid business partners (Danes and Olson, 2003; Hamilton, 2006). Clearly, the role expectations prevalent in the domestic domain often follow women into the family business (Salganicoff, 1990; Cole, 1997;

Hamilton, 2006). Although the roles undertaken may be subtle and lack formality they are nonetheless, important and are fundamental to the running of the family firm (Martinez Jimenez, 2009). In effect, despite being significant, women's contribution may go unrecognised and insufficiently rewarded in terms of salaries and job titles (Gillis-Donovan and Moynihan-Brandt, 1990). Moreover, although women may take an influential role in establishing and founding the venture, they are very rarely presented as leader, owner manager or entrepreneur.

Women in family firms are not immune to issues such as occupational segregation and discrimination which may affect their career advancement. However, in addition to these they may also face conflict over roles, family loyalties, relationships with parents and siblings and the primogeniture rule (Dumas, 1992; Rosenblatt et al., 1985; Martinez Jimenez, 2009). The term role conflict is often used to describe the often contradictory and competing roles within family–business dyads i.e. the expected family role (good mother and wife) and expected business role (professional worker) (Salganicoff, 1990; Cole, 1997). On occasions many women are prepared to sacrifice their own career advancement in order to minimise any potential role conflict (Marshack, 1993; Baines and Wheelock, 2000). One of the greatest challenges faced by such women is the combining of family and professional responsibilities (Cole, 1997; Vera and Dean, 2005). This conflict is often compounded by conflicting messages such as 'dedicate yourself fully to the business, but give the family children'; 'Do not take business home, but let's talk shop tonight' (Salganicoff, 1990: 133). So, women in family businesses are often trapped in this double bind (Hollander and Bukowitz, 1990: 145). Furthermore, the stereotypical, institutional impacts of gendered subordination are evident within family businesses (Salganicoff, 1990) and are instrumental in keeping women within such contexts invisible (Rowe and Hong, 2000). This often results in men assuming the manager/entrepreneur position whilst women play a supporting role such as bookkeeping in addition to taking full responsibility for domestic and family duties (Dumas, 1989; Hamilton, 2006). This supporting often 'behind the scenes' role has resulted in the term invisible women (Hollander and Bukowitz, 1990); in fact, invisibility is a particular issue for wives, where there is an assumption that the position held is due to them being married to the boss (Cole, 1997). According to Poza and Messer (2001: 34) 'whether spouses are in formal or informal positions, recognised or unrecognised for their contributions, they often adopt a role that seeks to preserve and strengthen family unity and the feasibility of family business continuity'. In addition, women play an important role in instilling the values of the firm to their children – the next generation of leaders (Martinez Jimenez, 2009).

Family business research reflects the masculine tone of the wider entrepreneurial discourse serving to reinforce the invisibility of women (Gillis-Donovan and Moynihan-Bradt, 1990; Hamilton, 2006; Philbrick and Fitzgerald, 2007). Unsurprisingly, such invisibility has resulted in difficulties inherent in accurately measuring women's contribution to family business (Vera and Dean, 2005). As Sharma (2004: 14) notes:

> no systematic research has yet been directed towards understanding the contextual and individual factors that buoy these women into leadership positions, their performance goals in terms of family and business dimensions, or the leadership and managerial styles adopted by them, pointing toward an interesting and ripe area for serious study.

Even though women's contribution to family businesses is significant (Cole, 1997), the media often represents such women as exceptions or novel. With Salganicoff (1990: 127) noting 'unfortunately, newspapers and magazines often like to print articles about the 'little girl' who became a successor in a family business, about how the devastated widow rescued her late husband's business or about how the little sister became more successful than her older brother in an automobile dealership'.

5.9 SUCCESSION

Women's increasing involvement in family business challenges the primogeniture rule whereby leadership of the business is transferred to the first born son (Barnes, 1988; Kepner, 1988; Dumas, 1989). Women are rarely seen as serious contenders for succession and are only considered as appropriate successors (leaders) in situations of crisis or when there are no suitable male heirs (Dumas, 1989; Curimbaba, 2002). Consequently, there are greater instances where daughters are unprepared and have received less encouragement and training to participate in leadership roles in the family business in comparison to their brothers or sons (Rosenblatt et al., 1985; Howorth and Assaraf Ali, 2001; Sharma, 2004). Traditional expectations regarding the role of women may in part help explain why daughters are often overlooked when it comes to leadership roles in family firms (Cole, 1997). The roles within father–daughter dyads include, the invisible successor, daddy's little girl, the silent voice and caretaker of the king's gold (Dumas, 1989). However, daughters often face specific challenges as a result of sceptical fathers and siblings, who have doubts regarding their ability and competence (Barnes, 1988).

Unsurprisingly, most women do not consider joining the family firm as a viable career option (Dumas, 1992). In a study conducted by Salganicoff (1990) only 27 per cent of the sample wanted to join the family business. In addition, such women were unlikely to view positions held as a professional career. However, access to industrial sectors such as construction and engineering which are often considered difficult and male oriented are often cited as one of the main advantages for women within family firms in addition to flexible working patterns and job security (Barnett and Barnett, 1988; Cole, 1997).

BOX 5.1 OVELLE PHARMACEUTICAL – WHEN THE DAUGHTER TAKES OVER

Founded in 1934, Ovelle Pharmaceutical is a privately owned family business based in Dundalk, Co. Louth, Ireland. The company had always been viewed as a small owner-managed business, manufacturing old fashioned, unbranded traditional creams and lotions, such as calamine lotion, Silcock's base and emulsifying ointments. Such products were typically sold over the counter by pharmacists all over the country and were highly regarded by GPs.

Joanna Gardiner only became involved in her father's business in 2000, when the company was for the most part seen as small and static, content to continue servicing its existing markets without deliberate expansion. Joanna's role to that point had been mainly marketing and promotion, a role she envisaged retaining for the foreseeable future. However, shortly after Joanna joined the company, Ovelle underwent a major restructuring. Staffing levels were reduced and a strategy developed to refocus the business as a sales-led organisation. To fund the planned restructuring, two local private investors were secured, in addition to funding from Enterprise Ireland. This resulted in the company moving from a family-owned business run by her father, Sean Gardiner, to a company with significant external shareholding. Joanna played a major role in the restructuring process and, in 2002, was appointed Managing Director.

Under Joanna's direction, Ovelle's new challenges would include growing the export business and introducing a branded skincare product line. With an increase in skin complaints such as eczema, psoriasis and dry skin, Joanna saw an opportunity to produce irritant-free pharmaceutical products that were not damaging to the skin. Another key challenge for Joanna involved bringing the company from a turnover of around €2m with a loss of €0.3m, to a profitable, growth-oriented operation.

Source: Ernst and Young Entrepreneur of the
Year Case Series 2007: 54–55.

5.10 COPRENEURSHIP

Copreneurs is a subset of family business and is the fastest-growing segment of small business activity (Marshack, 1993; Stewart-Gross and Stewart-Gross, 2007). Married couples who share ownership, management and responsibility for a business are known as co-entrepreneurial couples or 'copreneurs' (Marshack,

1994, 1998; Lewis and Massey, 2011) which results in a dyadic, committed relationship based on emotional ties and trust with a marked division of labour and responsibilities (De Bruin and Lewis, 2004). It is estimated to be an important growing business form (De Bruin and Lewis, 2004) with copreneurs representing over 30 per cent of all family businesses in the United States (Fitzgerald and Muske, 2002). However, it is difficult to estimate the exact number of such businesses, as many copreneurs choose to list their business as a sole proprietorship. The popularity of the copreneur phenomenon may be that in the early stages of business set up, family and business finances are linked and due to the economic bonds of marriage, a spouse automatically becomes a critical stakeholder in the family business (Steier and Greenwood, 2000; Aldrich and Cliff, 2003; Ruef et al., 2003). In a more informal way, entrepreneurs often consult with, and are influenced by, their spouses (Aldrich and Cliff, 2003), especially in the initial years of a new venture when the spouse can offer not only emotional support (Puhakka, 2002) but also personal and/or temporal resources (Baines and Wheelock, 2000; Danes and Olson, 2003). Copreneurship is prevalent in occupational contexts such as farming (Amarapurkar and Danes, 2005) which tie couples in their work together or where one spouse is active in the vocation of their partner (Zablocki and Kanter, 1976).

A common team composition is that of the husband and wife (or mixed-sex life partners) (Cachon, 1990), where the woman undertakes an ancillary role in the business domain, performing administrative and basic bookkeeping activities (Marshack, 1998; Firkin et al., 2003; Dupuis and De Bruin, 2004). Indeed, within the copreneurial team, Lucaccini and Muscat (2001: 6) suggest that 'the copreneurial husband tends to be the primary business decision maker, although the wife is an equal partner overall, sharing the activities and responsibilities of the firm'. Marshack (1998) and Firkin et al. (2003) found that the wives/female partners tacitly support the business effort by also taking sole responsibility for domestic labour and related caring responsibilities, absolving the male business owner from such activities. Whilst this gendered division of labour is commonplace in most households regardless of the economic activity of the male partner (Bradley, 2007) it is noted that where men are business owners, there is an assumption regarding the unpaid contributions of women not only as domestic labourers but also as invisible, unpaid business partners (Marshack, 1994; Mulholland, 1996; Hamilton, 2006; Lewis and Massey, 2011). Consequently, entrepreneurial couples who work closely together 'are often trapped by a gender-based division of responsibilities and authority' typically resulting 'in the wife acquiescing to [the husband's] benevolent authority' (Marshack, 1998: 169). It is accepted within the literature that copreneurs have an unequal division of task (Fitzgerald and Muske, 2002; Fairlie and Robb, 2008). Clarifying personal and business goals requires couples to define complementary work roles and respect boundaries between business and personal lives (Tompson and Tompson, 2000). Perhaps the most

BOX 5.2   CASE STUDY: AN EXAMPLE OF COPRENEURSHIP: JOINTLY OWNED AU PAIR AGENCY

The idea	The partnership	Implementation of idea
Originator of idea: the wife – Rosie	Rosie is 24 yrs and lead entrepreneur	Founded in 2006
Being a former au pair inspired the venture	Husband, Jim, is 28 yrs, employed as a marketing manager for an IT company; Chief Operating Officer in venture	Currently 12 employees and 18 months in operation
Encouraged and supported by her husband Jim		Second office opened in Dec 2009
	Both are directors and owners of the business, with Rosie having the majority share	Responsibilities: *Rosie*: Full-time; day-to-day responsibilities including dealing with clients and customers
	Family situation: currently no children	*Jim*: Part-time; strategic planning; managing finances and negotiations
		Eventually plan to adopt a franchising business model

challenging factor for copreneurs to contend with is the fact that they are in pursuit of 'two concurrent life goals that often make contradictory demands' (Tompson and Tompson, 2000: 2).

There is some evidence to indicate that the 'copreneurial husband tends to be the primary business decision maker although the wife is an equal partner in sharing the activities and responsibilities of the firm' (Lucaccini and Muscat, 2001: 6). The extant literature regarding copreneurship (Smith, 2000; Steier and Greenwood, 2000; Ruef *et al.*, 2003; Aldrich and Cliff, 2003) adopts a normative approach to the analysis of gendered roles; the assumption being that men occupy key entrepreneurial roles and women act as invisible handmaidens to the greater cause. However, a traditional gendered ordering within copreneurial businesses is not uniform; there is evidence that women are increasingly assuming the role of lead entrepreneur within copreneurial ventures (Koss-Feder, 2001; Poza and Messer, 2001; McAdam and Marlow, 2012). Lucaccini and Muscat (2001: 9) attribute this growth to 'corporate down-sizing, a return to pre-industrial values regarding family life, a belief in the equality of the sexes and a desire for greater control of one's own life'. However, little is known concerning the dynamics of copreneurial relationships which represent a reversal of normative gendered partnership roles although increasing numbers of women are undertaking the role of entrepreneurial leader (Danes and Olsen, 2003; McAdam and Marlow, 2012). Accordingly Tompson and Tompson (2000) refer to copreneurship as a much neglected area of research with Hamilton (2006: 256) concurring with this opinion; she argues that the current focus of debate 'commonly reflects and reinforces the relative silence and invisibility of women in entrepreneurial discourse. Embedded in that discourse is the assumption that the leadership involved in founding and running a business is most naturally male'.

5.11 SUMMARY

The trade off between work status and family commitments is of particular significance for women. Women's positioning within self-employment (i.e. part-time, home-based) merely reflects and reproduces these embedded socio-economic norms. Thus, family responsibilities continue to have an impact on the extent to which women engage with the labour market and entrepreneurship and thus their experiences of both differ compared to those of men. Within the wider entrepreneurship literature, there is evidence to support that entrepreneurship is male gendered and as a concept has masculine connotations. This is also reflected in the family business arena, where women not only engage in gendered stereo-typical roles within the business but where their contribution is also often unpaid and invisible. Furthermore, women often support the continuance of the male entrepreneurial leader whilst at the same time creating conditions whereby they challenged patriarchal norms. However, this only serves to reinforce and perpetuate entrepreneurship as a male construct and limits our understanding of entrepreneurship and entrepreneurial endeavour.

5.12 DISCUSSION POINTS

- Discuss the impact of the 'double shift' on the time and effort expended by women when it comes to entrepreneurial activity.
- Identify the hidden and often unpaid roles undertaken by women within a family business.
- Using relevant examples, discuss the role of the media in presenting women as legitimate business owners.

Chapter 6

Non-financial entrepreneurial capital

6.1 INTRODUCTION

It is recognised that those entrepreneurs who draw upon a broad and deep range of financial, human, social and symbolic capital create and grow more sustainable ventures. However, the nature and composition of entrepreneurial capital differs with gender; men and women launch their ventures with differing amounts of entrepreneurial capital and such differences may influence the performance of their ventures. It has been well documented that those entering self-employment usually do so from prior employment where they accumulate many of the resources necessary to commence a new venture. This chapter commences with an overview of the impact of the social context on the accrual of the range of predominately non-financial resources required to support the establishment, survival and growth of a new venture.

6.2 LEARNING OBJECTIVES

On completion of this chapter, students should be able to:

1 Describe and analyse the non-financial resources involved in the start-up process.
2 Critique entrepreneurial capital as a theoretical concept used to advance understanding of business start-up.
3 Understand the importance of entrepreneurial capital accrual in launching and growing sustainable ventures.

6.3 ENTREPRENEURIAL CAPITAL ACCRUAL

The variety and amount of capital possessed by entrepreneurs has been found to impact on both experiences of business ownership and firm performance (Kepler and Shane, 2007). According to Firkin (2003: 65) entrepreneurial capital is 'the total capital that an individual possesses'. Building on the resource-based view of the firm and borrowing from Bourdieu's Theories of Practice (Bourdieu, 1977), the concept of entrepreneurial capital has emerged in recognition of the need for entrepreneurs to accrue financial, human, social and symbolic capital in order to succeed (Davidsson and Honig, 2003; Firkin, 2003). Furthermore, it is agreed that the acquisition and development of entrepreneurial capital is initiated largely during experiences of the labour market prior to entering business ownership and the close proximity of appropriate role models (Storey, 1994; Hundley, 2001b); acknowledging this, women's accrual of entrepreneurial capital has to be contextualised within the wider socio-economic milieu (Marlow, 2002; Carter et al., 2007).

In respect to the acquisition of entrepreneurial capital, as noted above, a number of enduring market trends restrict the variety and amount of such capital possessed by, and available to women. Discontinuous work patterns and/or having to leave the labour market early due to discrimination or the glass ceiling effect may result in women having lower levels of human capital in comparison to men (Carter and Shaw, 2006). Occupational segregation also impacts upon women's ability to accrue substantive forms of entrepreneurial capital which in turn, limits their credibility as business owners and so, devalues their symbolic capital. Thus, in comparison with their male counterparts, women-owned businesses at start-up are undercapitalised with regards to financial, human and social capital (Carter et al., 2001). Consequently, the long-term impact on structural disadvantages and the resultant resource deficit on the performance and sustainability of women-owned businesses is of concern (Brush, 1992; Boden and Nucci, 2000). The extent to which men and women launch businesses from the same initial levels of capitalisation with regards, financial, human and social capital is the basis on which the so-called 'female under-performance hypotheses' is challenged (Carter and Shaw, 2006).

6.4 HUMAN CAPITAL

Human capital is the knowledge and skills acquired through education, managerial experiences and industrial knowledge (Becker, 1964; Davidsson and Honig, 2003). However, some go further and argue that it incorporates all traits and abilities that can be used to enable someone to be economically productive within society (Shanahan and Tuma, 1994). Moreover, such skills are not fixed but rather can be learned and developed (Gibb, 1993, 2000; Athayde, 2009). Individuals are able to increase their knowledge as a result of formal education (i.e. university education), informal education (i.e. work experience) and non-formal education (adult education) (Davidsson and Honig, 2003). In turn, it is not surprising that there is a positive relationship between human capital and effective entrepreneurial activity; as such, activity is influenced by the resources acquired through education and work experience (Jones et al., 2010; Teece, 2011). In fact, there is evidence to suggest that not only is the likelihood of becoming an entrepreneur correlated to higher levels of human capital (Arenius and Minniti, 2005), but once launched sufficient human capital resources can lead to higher performance in subsequent ventures (Hitt et al., 2001).

6.5 FINANCIAL CAPITAL

Financial capital is considered to be a leveraging resource due to its ability to secure other resources (Brush et al., 2001b) and also a buffering mechanism in times of uncertainty and crisis (Copper et al., 1994). In respect to the acquisition of financial capital, a number of enduring labour market trends can be identified which restrict the variety and amount of such capital possessed by, and available to, women. The persistence of the gender pay gap, limited career progression and fragmented working patterns combine to constrain women's opportunities to amass personal funds for investment purposes (Marlow et al., 2008; Women and Equality Unit, 2008). Such factors certainly limit the accrual of financial capital but also spill over into the opportunity to accumulate the human (education and experience) and social capital (contacts and networks) necessary to inform new venture creation (Brindley, 2005; Shaw et al., 2005). This argument has been supported by empirical research which confirms that despite the generic challenges faced by all who found and launch new ventures, there are gender related constraints regarding the accrual of formal and informal capital and that this disadvantage is reflected in women's accumulation of, demand for and use of business finance (Verheul and Thurik, 2001; Fraser, 2005; Roper and Scott, 2007). Support for this assertion arises from research which finds that women are more likely to draw upon limited personal savings to finance their businesses and are generally reluctant to seek formal, external debt or equity investment (Greene et al., 1999; Roper and Scott, 2007). Constrained investment strategies then inform the argument that women are risk averse within the entrepreneurial field (Ahl, 2004; Kepler and Shane, 2007). However, such undercapitalisation must be sited within the entrepreneurial context, which is perceived to have high levels of risk (Marlow, 2010); and as such is a rational response.

6.6 SOCIAL CAPITAL

Much of the evidence pertaining to social capital is based on the assumption 'that social structure is a kind of capital that can create for certain individuals a competitive advantage in pursuing their ends' (Burt, 2000: 4). As a result, the development of social capital is widely acknowledged as vital during the early stages of new venture creation (Aldrich and Zimmer, 1986; Uzzi, 1997; Battisti and McAdam, 2012). Consequently, entrepreneurs not only have to build partnerships and network relations, but they must also ensure that the emerging social structure meets their resource needs (Portes, 1998; Battisti and McAdam, 2012).

55

BOX 6.1 LILIAS CRUIKSHANK: ENTREPRENEUR'S GENERAL HUMAN CAPITAL

Lilias Cruikshank left school at 16 with no formal qualifications. She was able to work her way up the managerial ladder in a variety of recruitment consultancies. At the age of 44, Lilias was made redundant from her managerial role in a management recruitment agency, which was a highly competitive industry. She decided to start her own business rather than seek an employment position. Lilias believed that she had accumulated considerable industry-specific and managerial know-how, and that she had the personal skills to run a people-related business. Her sister-in-law, with no prior ownership experience, was a nursery nurse who also wanted to work for herself. Lilias decided to start a nursery day-care business using her sister-in-law's industry related expertise. With the pooling of their accumulated managerial knowledge and talents, Lilias believed that they had sufficient resources to establish and run an efficient and professionally managed nursery business.

Source: Westhead, P., Ucbasarn, D., Wright, M. and Martin, F. (2003) *Habitual Entrepreneurs in Scotland*. Glasgow: Scottish Enterprise, cited in Westhead *et al.* (2011: 250).

For this reason it is important to distinguish between social network and social capital, as this distinguishes structure from function. A network becomes social capital for an actor, not as a result of its structure but because of its function and associated benefits (Shaw, 2006). As social capital results from interaction and is embedded in relations between different actors, it is complex to describe. Relations may be formal or informal, strong or weak (Granovetter, 1973, 1985), vertical or horizontal (Putnam, 1993), bonding or bridging (Woolcock, 1998; Putnam, 1995). Social capital according to Nahapiet and Ghosal (1998: 107) is the 'resources individuals obtained from knowing others, being part of a network with them, or merely being known to them and having a good reputation'.

6.7 FEMALE NETWORKING

It is interesting to note that whilst entrepreneurs may by characterised by their autonomy and independence, they are also very dependent on ties of trust and cooperation (McAdam and Marlow, 2007). The entrepreneur's ability to construct and develop networks during early stages of start-up is crucial for entrepreneurial growth. In fact, networks do not emerge without considerable endeavour (Shaw, 2006). Networks of social ties reflect the initial stages of new venture start-up which thrive on innovative and creative thinking and an opportunity focus orientation. As the enterprise grows, these networks of personal contacts become the building blocks on which strong business relationships are formed/developed (Shaw, 2003, 2006). Networking provides significant advantages for female entrepreneurs including access to advice, information, strategic alliances and the acquisition of credibility and legitimacy for their ventures (Carter and Shaw, 2006; Linehan and Scullion, 2008).

However, variations occur in the process of networking and what networks are used for between male and female entrepreneurs (Aldrich, 1989; Carter *et al.*, 2001). In fact, Starr and Yudkin (1996: 40) note that 'the few studies that compare the networking activities of women and men business owners show differences in the sex composition of the networks of women, but not in how men and women use their networks'. The sex composition of networks does vary by gender (Carter *et al.*, 2001), with women tending to have networks composed entirely of other women, which they use for emotional support. Consequently, attention has been drawn to the limited diversity of female entrepreneurs' networks (Renzulli *et al.*, 2000; Foss, 2010) and often the phrase homophily is used to describe such member selection; with homophily referring 'to the selection of other team members on the basis of similar ascriptive characteristics, such as gender, ethnicity, nationality, appearance and the like' (Ruef *et al.*, 2003: 196).

Women form long-term relationships based on affective ties whilst men form short-term relationships based on weak ties (Minniti and Arenius, 2003). When it comes to networking activities, there is evidence to suggest that differences exist in the type of networks utilised by women and men as well as different priorities when establishing networks; with women tending to seek social advantages such as emotional support, compared with men who tend to seek personal advantages (Buttner, 1993). Female entrepreneurs seek to build and emphasise collaborative inclusive relationships (Martin, 2001) and are often regarded as 'soft networkers' (Foss, 2010: 92). In fact, according to Harrison and Mason (2007: 453) women in networks tend to provide emotional support and empathy whilst men focus on the transactional exchange of goods and services: 'women express – men repress'. There is also an assumption within the literature on gender and entrepreneurial networking, that women are disadvantaged as a result of their role in society and family and this has a detrimental effect on their networking activities (Foss, 2010). However, McGregor and Tweed (2002) warn against treating all women business owners as a homogeneous group, as there is more variation within than between the sexes when it comes to entrepreneurial networking.

6.8 FORMAL NETWORKING MECHANISMS

A key theme within the networking literature has been the importance of formal networking for women (Hampton *et al.*, 2009) especially in relation to compensating

57

BOX 6.2 COULD NETWORKING HELP YOU TO GROW YOUR BUSINESS?

Self-employed mum of two and Chair of the Maidenhead group, Claire Fryer tells us her story...

I decided to go it alone after having my second son and my chosen career of PR and Marketing meant I was able to work from home with minimum set-up and fit work in around school runs and nursery sessions. After a short time working as a solo freelancer One to Three Marketing Solutions was born – along with a great friend of mine Lisa Vassallo, who is a fellow marketer, we saw a gap in the market for the expertise we could offer and in February 2010 we took the plunge and set up in business together.

Speaking to friends and colleagues who had taken a similar leap of faith the advice to get out there and network cropped up time and time again. Everyone said it was a fantastic way to gain new clients, build your business and make invaluable business contacts. We were new to all of this and the thought of walking into a room full of strangers with a bundle of our shiny new business cards filled us with minor horror! After lots of background research, or attending a few different networking events and following recommendations Lisa and I decided to join the Women in Business Network and really have never looked back! We love attending the monthly business lunches that never fail to deliver new business leads, new contacts, a friendly welcome and a real sense of team that can get diluted if you work for yourself. Joining a networking group provides you with your own virtual office which helps to replace the infrastructure of working for a company

Effective networking

Networking is all about building relationships with other likeminded (in the case if WIBN) businesswomen. The monthly meetings are in a structured environment that allow for around 30 minutes of open networking, informally chatting to the other members and visitors. This is followed by a more formal monthly minute that gives everyone a chance to speak for 60 seconds about her business. Members are regularly invited to present a 5 minute spotlight which gives you the chance to go into more depth about your business – with one spotlight at each meeting it is often the talking point of the meeting! I know many people curl up into a ball at the thought of making a presentation, but speaking from my experience, everyone in my networking group is so supportive, you can remain seated if you'd prefer not to stand in front of the room. The only rule is – whatever makes you comfortable! After each meeting we are encouraged to organise separate 1-to-1 sessions which

give individuals the time to get to know each other better and fully understand their business. I always aim for at least one a month to keep my networking mind focused. This also then gives you access to a much wider
network, as once somebody gets to know you better they are then more likely
to recommend you to one of their friends or colleagues.

By Claire Fryer, *Families Magazine* (issue 59)

Source: http://www.wibn.co.uk/.

for any shortfalls within their own informal networking activities. This has
resulted in the development of formal structured women's networks exclusively
supporting female entrepreneurs (Donnellon and Langowitz, 2009). There is
some evidence to suggest that women business owners prefer to network with
other females and so choose to engage with and utilise women-only networks that
provide mutual support and confidence building opportunities (Buttner, 1993;
Prowess, 2003). This preference is based on the expectations that such networks
will provide a more supportive and encouraging environment than mixed networks (ibid.).

A perceived absence of formal structured women's networks (Fielden *et al.*,
2003; Klyver and Terjesen, 2007), combined with an inability to penetrate the
'old boys' club', is often cited as significant barriers to women's entrepreneurial
ambitions (Carter, 1993; Timberlake, 2005). Such exclusion is considered detrimental to women-owned businesses as these networks are considered to be an
important source of business opportunities (Gamba and Kleiner, 2001; Timberlake,
2005). Male type networking activities such as golf trips, lap dancing clubs often
exclude women (Fine, 2010). However, gaining access to these networks, beyond
mere tokenism poses real challenges for women due to concerns regarding low
self-confidence, self-efficacy, discrimination and the time and effort required to
engage in such networks given their domestic responsibilities (Marlow and Strange,
1994; Shaw *et al.*, 2001). Therefore, it is necessary to consider women's networking as an activity centred upon the intersection of work, family and social life
(Ibarra, 1993; Foss, 2010).

6.9 SYMBOLIC CAPITAL

Symbolic capital is an intangible source of power (Bourdieu, 1990) that captures
'the capacity that systems of meaning and signification have of shielding and
thereby strengthening, relations of oppression and exploitation by hiding them
under the cloak of nature, benevolence and meritocracy' (Wacqaunt, 1993: 1–2).
Symbolic capital refers to, though not limited to reputation, credibility and legitimacy (De Clercq and Voronov, 2009c). For nascent entrepreneurs, symbolic

capital enables them to articulate an image synonymous with entrepreneurship such as risk taking and competitiveness. There are considerable uncertainties for stakeholders when assessing the market value of new ventures given the liabilities of newness and smallness (Stinchcombe, 1965) with symbolic capital acting to reduce this uncertainty through the articulation of positive signs which signal durability and growth. New entrepreneurs often lack the familiarity and credibility enjoyed by more established entrepreneurs and as such portraying sustainability and profitability is an important aspect of the legitimation process (De Clercq and Voronov, 2009a, 2009b, 2011). Entrepreneurs must focus on 'framing the unknown in such a way that it becomes believable' (Aldrich and Fiol, 1994: 651). In order to convince stakeholders of their venture's merit, entrepreneurs must demonstrate institutional legitimacy in that they fit with the entrepreneurial image and play by field rules yet, they must also demonstrate innovative legitimacy, in that their idea is sufficiently novel (De Clercq and Voronov, 2009a). Women entrepreneurs face more challenges in achieving this balance and establishing legitimacy than their male counterparts (Pinson and Jinnett, 1992).

6.10 SUMMARY

Within the literature differences in entrepreneurial rates between men and women have been explained through the accrual and exploitation of entrepreneurial capital. Therefore, within this chapter the non-financial aspects of entrepreneurial capital such as human capital, social capital and symbolic capital have been explored. It is evident that women's previous experience in the labour market plays a critical role in the accrual of appropriate resources necessary for launching and growing sustainable ventures. This accrual is also aided by the close proximity of appropriate role models. In order to fully understand the challenges faced by female entrepreneurs, their accrual of entrepreneurial capital must be contextualised within the wider socio-economic milieu.

6.11 DISCUSSION POINTS

- Discuss the impact of the close proximity of role models on women's accrual of entrepreneurial capital.
- Is networking a competency that you are born with or can it be nurtured and developed? Discuss.
- Discuss the importance of 'fitting in' whilst 'standing out' in the context of gaining entrepreneurial legitimacy. Give examples to justify your answer.

Chapter 7

Financing women-owned businesses

7.1 INTRODUCTION

In this chapter the challenges faced by women when it comes to financing their ventures are discussed commencing with an overview of the demand and supply of finance required to support sustainable ventures. This will then be followed by a discussion of the key issues pertinent to women such as the so-called risk aversity of women, gender stereotyping and discrimination practices of financial institutions. The chapter concludes with a spotlight on the Diana Project International (formerly known as the Diana Project), a US research initiative established to investigate the growth models pursued by female entrepreneurs and the supply and demand of venture capital.

7.2 LEARNING OBJECTIVES

On completion of this chapter, students should be able to:

1 Recognise the challenges faced by female entrepreneurs when it comes to financing their ventures.
2 Understand such challenges from both a demand and supply side perspective.
3 Challenge the myths and stereotypical assumptions associated with women and equity finance.

7.3 ACCESSING FINANCE

Accessing appropriate finance is a documented challenge for business owners per se; however, there is a well researched body of literature to indicate that female business owners experience additional disadvantages as a result of their gender (Bhide, 2000; Carter, 2000; Marlow and Patton, 2005). According to Hisrich (1985: 73) 'while financing is a problem for every entrepreneur, for women entrepreneurs the problem is even more acute'. This problem is

61

particularly significant given the importance of appropriate start-up capital in terms of sustainability, growth and performance (Mason and Harrison, 1992; Becker-Blease and Sohl, 2007). Persistent and consistent across countries, there is evidence to suggest that female entrepreneurs tend to use significantly smaller amounts of start-up capital than their male counterparts (Minniti et al., 2005). In their study in the United Kingdom, Carter and Rosa (1998) found that although men and women use similar sources to finance their ventures, female entrepreneurs rely on a third of the capital used by their male counterparts. The reasons as to why women use significantly less capital than men may be due to the fact that women are more likely to launch businesses out of necessity (Minniti et al., 2005), start businesses in low-capital intensive sectors (Orser et al., 2005), tend to be more risk averse (Marlow, 2010) and encounter discrimination in financing practices (Verheul and Thurik, 2001; Harrison and Mason, 2007). Moreover, they also command lower levels of funding, depend upon informal or more expensive sources of finance, in addition to relying on limited business networks (Thompson et al., 2009). Consequently, there are significant differences in the capital structure of male and female-owned businesses (Verheul and Thurik, 2001). Accordingly, women are more likely to start up businesses with lower levels of initial capitalisation, utilise lower ratio of debt finance and are less inclined to use private equity finance (Marlow and Patton, 2005). Initial undercapitalisation may have an impact on growth and subsequent performance (Carter and Allen, 1997) as a direct correlation has been made between starting capital and long-term performance of the firm (Watson, 2002). Accordingly, financial constraints and undercapitalisation is often presented as a reason for the underperformance of women-owned businesses (Orser et al., 2005; Coleman, 2007).

7.4 CHALLENGES FACED BY FEMALE ENTREPRENEURS

Despite the financing of female-owned businesses being the most researched area within female entrepreneurship (Gatewood et al., 2003; Orser et al., 2005; Harrison and Mason, 2007), there is still some conflicting evidence regarding the challenges faced by female entrepreneurs when it comes to raising finance (Carter et al., 2001). This debate is largely based on the lack of unequivocal evidence to support claims that women face credibility issues with lenders (Brush, 1992; Mahoot, 1997; Carter and Rosa, 1998). In fact, Carter and Allen (2001) identified four areas where women may face difficulties when it comes to the financing process. First, women may be disadvantaged in their ability to raise start-up capital (Van Auken et al., 1993; Carter and Rosa, 1998). Second, women may have difficulties providing guarantees due to limited personal assets and credit rating (Hisrich and Brush, 1986; Riding and Swift, 1990). Third, they may face difficulties related to accessing informal financial networks to support the ongoing growth of their businesses (Aldrich, 1989). Finally, issues related to gender

Table 7.1 *Bootstrapping strategies used by female entrepreneurs in 2011*

Delayed purchases	71.3%
Delayed compensation of business owners	64.9%
Credit cards	64.9%
Personal savings	55.3%
Delayed hiring	54.3%
Asked for discounts from service providers	35.1%
Line of credit	35.1%
Creative compensation e.g. bartering, making non-cash payments like company stock	27.70%
Vendor or customer financing	22.30%
Bank loans	19.20%
Loans from family and friends	17.02%
Sold receivables	6.40%

Source: Center for Women's Business Research, February 2012. W-Biz Insight Research Panel.

stereotyping and discrimination (Greene *et al.*, 2001). Existence of gendered stereotypes can actually act as a barrier to women securing finance as they feed negative assumptions about the relationship between women and entrepreneurship. Whether female entrepreneurs apply to an institutional financier (a bank, a finance agency), a friend, a relative or even her spouse, they are likely to come up against the assumption that 'women can't handle money' (Bruni *et al.*, 2004a: 262). In France for example, a married women was not allowed to open a credit account without her husband's consent until 1965 (Veil, 1994). Furthermore, it was not until 1975, that the Equal Credit Opportunity Act was passed in the United States. Table 7.1 sets out the 'bootstrapping strategies' used by female entrepreneurs (center for Women's Business Research, 2012).

7.5 PECKING ORDER HYPOTHESIS

The majority of women-owned businesses are financed by personal savings (love money), family and friends, credit cards and some bank finance (Brush *et al.*, 2006). There is evidence to suggest that business owners regardless of gender have preferences for personal savings including contributions from family and friends and bank lending (Marlow and Patton, 2005). These preferences seemed to be more predominant in women as the debt-risk aversion appears to be stronger in this group (Kepler and Shane, 2007). When it comes to the capital structure supporting entrepreneurial ventures, Myer's (1984) Pecking Order of Capital Structure Theory explains the preferential treatment given by entrepreneurs to certain types of funding at different times. This is also what Harrison and Mason (2000) referred to as the 'pipeline' model, whereby business owners will approach the four main sources in the following order. First, personal savings as well as investment from family and friends; second, debt financing, which is normally bank finance although it can also include hire purchase and leasing; third, government grants and finally venture capital and informal/private equity (Jarvis, 2000). Funding is sought in a hierarchical pattern, commencing with informal sources followed by bank finance and then equity funding (Cassar, 2001).

7.6 BANK FINANCE

Banks are the critical source of external funding (Verheul and Thurik, 2001; Marlow and Patton, 2005) for small firms. According to Mirchandani (1999) female entrepreneurs' creditability and legitimacy, when it comes to securing bank loans, is influenced by the age and size of their business in addition to the industrial sector. Socio-economic positioning whereby women launch businesses which they can keep small and manage from home with little start-up capital will evidently impact on their funding requirements (Marlow, 2002). However, women are more likely to be discouraged borrowers as they perceive that they will be rejected when they apply for bank funding (Kon and Storey, 2003; Hill et al., 2006; Roper and Scott, 2007); this may in part explain the less likelihood of women applying for credit (Orser et al., 2005).

Discriminatory practices have been cited as one reason for female entrepreneurs' difficulties in securing debt finance (Carter et al., 2001). Although more anecdotal and of an individualised nature, there is some evidence of the existence of discriminatory practices in the interactions between bank managers and female entrepreneurs (McKechnie et al., 1998). However, many bank managers refute the claim of gender bias and state that they are only interested in the entrepreneurial profile, male or female (Orhan, 2001). In fact, banks' refusal of loans is attributed to discrimination rather than poorly constructed business plans (Buttner and Rosen, 1992). However, women may obtain credit under less favourable conditions in comparison to their male equivalents (Coleman, 2000). This is supported by Fraser (2005) who found evidence of women being asked for higher levels of collateral and/or being charged higher interest rates on loans compared with male entrepreneurs.

Evidently, bank lending policies and procedures may disadvantage or discriminate against women (Carter and Shaw, 2006). However, rather than discriminating against women as a group, it appears that it is the size, age and industrial sector of their ventures that contributes to their inability to secure bank finance. According to Coleman (2000: 49) 'banks discriminate on the basis of firm size, preferring to lend to larger and one would assume more established firms'. Furthermore, Fay and Williams (1993: 65) state 'bank staff are not guilty of discrimination in such situations, rather applicants' socialization and work related experiences have disadvantaged them compared to male applicants'. However, difficulties faced by women when raising finance may well be the result of their failure to conform to the normative entrepreneurial image (male) as opposed to discriminatory practices by finance providers (Bruni *et al.*, 2004a). Added to this, bank managers' perceptions of female entrepreneurs may 'reflect men's inability to split the feminine image into two: a woman and person; the business woman wanted to be treated just like any other person, but for most bank managers "any other person" means a man' (Hertz, 1986: 191). Thus, women may not fit the stereotypical image of the ideal entrepreneur (Ahl, 2004) and so are under constant pressure to demonstrate their entrepreneurial ability (Orhan, 2001). In fact, studies focusing on bank managers' perceptions of entrepreneurs confirmed that male entrepreneurs scored higher on characteristics affiliated with successful entrepreneurship than female entrepreneurs (Buttner and Rosen, 1992; Carter and Allen, 1997). Although Buttner and Rosen's (1992) study supported the existence of gendered stereotypes amongst bank managers' evaluation of business plans, there was no evidence to support the influence of such stereotypes on their lending decisions. Evidence with regards to discrimination in financing practices is mixed due to the difficultly in the attainment of reliable data thus making it difficult to unequivocally support claims that supply-side discriminatory practices are prevalent (Carter *et al.*, 2007). Thus, although gender matters (Alsos *et al.*, 2006), it would be wrong to conclude that women's restricted access to debt finance particularly bank loans is solely the result of discriminatory practices (Orhan, 2001).

7.7 DEMAND-SIDE RISK AVERSION

In addition to issues related to the supply of finance, there also appears to be debt aversion among female entrepreneurs. In fact, there is a significant body of evidence which represents women as risk averse and as having a lower propensity towards risk than men especially when making financial decisions (Minniti, 2009). So, for example, evidence drawn from a range of academic disciplines and enacted scenarios supports the notion that young males have the highest degrees of risk tolerance whilst women of all ages exhibit risk avoidance (Byrnes *et al.*, 1999; Kepler and Shane, 2007). Drawing upon evolutionary analyses as explanatory devices (Kaplan and Hill, 1985; Smith and Bird, 2001), it is suggested that women's traditional protective parenting role, their socialisation as carers and nurturers and greater vulnerability to violence has discouraged risk taking, embedded within a greater sensitivity to loss and so, promotes risk avoidance. Thus, women are portrayed as cautious borrowers with a preference for informal funding (Fraser, 2005; Carter and Shaw, 2006). This finding remains constant even when variables such as business size and sector are manipulated (Watson, 2002; Hill *et al.*, 2006; Carter *et al.*, 2007; Roper and Scott, 2007).

Accordingly, femininity and risk aversity become interlinked; this association is deemed problematic as it informs women's reluctance to use formal financial products or to seek higher levels of investment to support sustainable start-ups and to promote future growth (Marlow and Patton, 2005). As a result of a supposed lower tolerance to risk, women are believed to prefer the less risky option of higher safety as opposed to higher profits (Watson and Robinson, 2003; Kepler and Shane, 2007). In fact, the extant evidence regarding women and entrepreneurial risk taking portrays women as disadvantaged. So for example, Brush *et al.* (2006) found that women had a preference for businesses with lower failure probabilities and were less willing to exchange gain for risk, in addition to spending more time and effort minimising risk. However, the idea that women are more risk averse than men has been contested by those who claim that women's risk aversity must be sited within the entrepreneurial context which is perceived to have high levels of risk and as such is a rational response (Sonfield *et al.*, 2001; McGregor and Tweed, 2002; Marlow, 2010).

7.8 VENTURE CAPITAL

Although gender differences in securing debt finance have been given considerable attention (Buttner and Rosen, 1988; Riding and Swift, 1990; Coleman, 2000; Orser *et al.*, 2005), less attention has been paid to women's experiences of accessing external equity finance (Mason and Harrison, 2000; Brush *et al.*, 2001a). Within the area of gender and venture equity finance, there is a dominance of research that relies on US samples (Hill *et al.*, 2006), leading to calls for more research which explores the experiences of women business owners in other geographical regions (Orser *et al.*, 2005) as findings from US samples may not be directly transferable or reflective of other contextual settings (Ahl, 2004; Harrison and Mason, 2007). Whilst there are acknowledged disadvantages associated with equity funding such as constraints upon entrepreneurial prerogative and pressure to expand sales and market share (Busenitz *et al.*, 2004; Wijbenga and Postma, 2007), the benefits are well documented. The importance of venture capital is noted by Bygrave *et al.* (2002: 105): 'entrepreneurs are the engines that drive new companies and financing is the fuel that drives them. Hence, financial support, especially equity finance for starting a company, is an important entrepreneurial framework condition'. Venture capital investment supports early stage growth (Barney *et al.*, 1996; De Bruin and Flint-Hartle, 2005) with such firms achieving higher survival rates and leading roles in product and process innovation (Sandberg, 1986; Feldman, 2001; Franke *et al.*, 2006). Despite this recognition, in all of the GEM countries combined, approximately only 15,000 companies were funded in 2008 compared to tens of millions that were funded by informal investment. As such, the likelihood of raising venture capital is very rare; in fact evidence indicates that fund managers only invest in approximately 5 per cent of the opportunities presented to them (Berlin, 1998). Interestingly, it is claimed that in the United States, 'a person has a higher chance of winning a million dollars or more in a state lottery than getting venture capital to launch a new venture' (GEM, 2009: 57).

Women are less likely to apply for venture capital funding than their male counterparts (Orser et al., 2005); thus, a gender gap/disparity exists when it comes to securing venture capital (Morris et al., 2006). Although women-owned businesses account for 30 per cent of businesses in the United States, less than 5 per cent are financed by venture capital funding (Brush et al., 2002). Of those women who are successful, they on average obtain significantly lower amounts of venture capital than their male counterparts (Gatewood et al., 2003). According to Greene et al. (2001) reasons for women's difficulty in securing venture capital include the structural barriers faced by women in this process, women's aversion to such finance (as there is evidence to suggest that women may value the retention control more than men) (Cliff, 1998), and women's lack of human capital which is deemed necessary by such finance providers. Furthermore, venture capitalists traditionally are attracted to high technology sectors which have the promise of high return; as women's businesses tend to be located in the retail and service sectors, they may not be of interest to venture capitalists (Brush et al., 2001b). And although women may be found in high technology start-up teams they are however, 'noticeably absent from the leadership positions in venture-funded start-ups' (Brush et al., 2001b: 1).

Furthermore, women's reduced time spent within the labour market, coupled with industrial experience gained predominately in the retail and service sectors may diminish their credibility when it comes to accessing equity finance (Boden and Nucci, 2000). In fact, Carter et al. (2003) found that human capital (graduate education) influenced an entrepreneur's ability to gain venture capital funding; with human capital referring to resources acquired as a result of education, managerial experience and industrial sector knowledge (Teece, 2011). Another reason cited for women's lack of engagement with venture capital may be inadequate networking, as this is an important catalyst in the successful acquiring of venture capital (Becker-Blease and Sohl, 2007). The preference by women to have female-dominated networks coupled with the male dominance of the venture capital industry diminishes the likelihood of women's networks overlapping with venture capitalists (Gatewood et al., 2009); therefore access may be difficult without appropriate networks and gatekeepers. In effect, it is likely that women will have difficulties gaining access to key individuals who may be influential in helping them secure equity funding (Manolova et al., 2007).

7.9 BUSINESS ANGELS

Research on equity finance has predominantly focused on venture capital finance; however, business angel finance is a critical source of venture capital especially at the seed and start-up stages (Mason and Harrison, 1999; Brush et al., 2002).

Business angels are typically high net worth individuals who provide risk capital, in addition to providing a new venture with focus, credibility, networks, experience and expertise (Mason and Harrison, 1999; Becker-Blease and Sohl, 2007). In fact, access to the business angel's 'gold plated rolodex' is often regarded as the key difference between venture capitalist and business angel finance (Amatucci and Sohl, 2004). Such capital is often regarded as the important preliminary stage of securing formal venture capital (Freear and Wetzel, 1992; Mason and Harrison, 2000). Despite this importance, business angels are notoriously difficult to identify and prefer to remain on the margins of the investment community (Mason and Harrison, 1999). Consequently, there has been a paucity of research with regard to women's access to angel financing (Mason and Harrison, 2000). According to Brush et al. (2004: 56) 'although finding and engaging angel investors is a challenge for anyone, women entrepreneurs have experienced particular difficulty'. In Becker-Blease and Sohl's (2007) comparative study investigating whether women and men have equal access to angel capital, the authors in fact found no significant differences in the percentage success rate of women (13.33 per cent) and men (14.79 per cent) obtaining capital investment. However, biological gender did emerge as a differentiator in the disproportionate share of applications made, with women only submitting 8.9 per cent of proposals within this sample.

Another study focusing on five women who had secured business angel finance by Amatucci and Sohl (2004), identified challenges in the process due to lender stereotyping assumptions regarding their ability as entrepreneurs despite their educational and work experience. The exploration of women's role in the supply (equity provider) and demand (equity seeker) of equity also identifies the limited number of female business angel investors (Mason and Harrison, 1992; Becker-Blease and Sohl, 2007). In fact, Harrison and Mason (2007) posit this figure to be approximately 5 per cent of all business angel investors. This is of significance, as there is evidence to support homophily within the business angel market, whereby entrepreneurs have a strong preference to submit proposals to angel investors of the same sex (Becker-Blease and Sohl, 2007). To conclude, the low proportion of women-owned businesses acquiring angel capital should be considered in relation to the low number of female entrepreneurs seeking such capital and the limited number of female business angel providers.

7.10 THE DIANA PROJECT

The gender gap in venture capital has been the driving force behind the Diana Project International, a research initiative set up to investigate growth models pursued by female entrepreneurs and the supply and demand of venture capital. According to Brush et al. (2001b), women are constrained by myths associated with their gender when it comes to attracting venture capital. The persistence of such myths and stereotypical assumptions may in some way explain why women's ability to secure

BOX 7.1   SPOTLIGHT ON THE DIANA PROJECT

The Diana Project is a research collaboration focused upon the study of female business owners and their business growth activities. The original purpose of the Diana Project was to investigate the apparent disconnects between the high growth potential of women owned businesses and the resources needed, particularly equity funding, to finance this growth.

There are two primary objectives:

1   To raise the awareness and expectations of women business owners around pursuing growth for their firms, and to educate these women about the characteristics of equity funded businesses and how the equity funding process works.
2   To increase recognition among equity capital providers about the advantages of investing in women owned businesses.

The Diana Project has expanded into the Diana Project International which is focused more broadly on scholarship regarding all types and forms of women's entrepreneurship and growth. Diana International serves as a convenor for researchers interested in this topic, holding bi-annual conferences in locations around the world. Diana International highlights high-growth, women-led ventures around the world. Currently more than 250 researchers from 37 countries and even more than 45 universities are involved in this consortium. Diana International has produced 7 International Conferences, 3 books and 7 Special Issues of Academic Journals. This research is used as an impetus and foundation for the implementation of policy, training and resources that help advance the state of practice of women entrepreneurs.

By Professor Candida Brush and Professor Patricia Greene

Source: http://www.gemconsortium.org/docs/download/768

equity finance is limited. These myths are the guiding framework used by the Diana Project International to explore the gender gap in equity financing strategies between male- and female-owned ventures. The Diana Project International claims 'that there is a substantial funding gap that limits woman's opportunities to grow their ventures aggressively and to lead high-value firms' (Brush *et al.*, 2002b: 1).

7.11 SUMMARY

Within female entrepreneurship, finance is the most researched area and as a consequence there is evidence to suggest that gender differences exist when it comes to raising external finance. Some of the reasons cited to account for such

BOX 7.2 EIGHT MYTHS ABOUT WOMEN AND EQUITY CAPITAL

1   Women *don't* want to own high growth businesses.
2   Women *don't* have the right *educational* backgrounds to build large ventures.
3   Women *don't* have the right types of experience to build large ventures.
4   Women *aren't* in the network and lack the social contacts to build a credible venture.
5   Women *don't* have the *financial savvy* or resources to start high growth businesses.
6   Women *don't* submit business plans to equity providers.
7   Women-owned ventures are *in industries* unattractive to venture capitalists.
8   Women are *not a force* in the venture capital industry.

Source: www.dianaproject.org

differences include the dominance of women-owned businesses in retail and service sectors, the risk aversity of women and gender stereotyping and discrimination. In fact, discrimination has been offered as a reason for undercapitalisation of women-owned businesses in relation to their male counterparts. However, the findings are mixed. In fact, there is little evidence of explicit discrimination and women's difficulties in raising finance may be more due to industrial sector (low growth and limited market expansion potential) and poorly constructed business plans rather than an outcome of their characteristics or their ability to run successful enterprises. More recently, greater attention has been paid to the challenges faced by women when securing equity finance. Although to date the majority of such research has focused on US samples, interesting insights have been provided into the gender equity finance gap. In fact, the question as to why so few women use venture capital to fund their ventures was the initial driving ethos behind the Diana Project International.

7.12 DISCUSSION POINTS

■   'Women are more risk averse than men.' Critically evaluate this statement using examples to justify your answer.
■   Identify ways in which women can effectively 'bootstrap' their ventures.
■   Select two of the eight myths identified in Box 7.2 and discuss their impact on women's attainment of equity capital.

Chapter 8

New sites of women's entrepreneurship: high technology entrepreneurship

8.1 INTRODUCTION

This chapter responds to calls for the investigation into the role of gendering in shaping and informing entrepreneurial decisions, industrial sectors and rates of entrepreneurial activity by exploring new sites of female entrepreneurship. Despite the positive perception of entrepreneurship in addition to the possibilities for greater flexibility and an escape from rigid career structures, women remain heavily underrepresented as Science, Engineering and Technology (SET) business owners. The limited presence of women business owners has commanded some interest and exploration prompting the development of a feminist critique relating to the prevailing masculinised culture within the high technology sector.

8.2 LEARNING OBJECTIVES

On completion of this chapter, students should be able to:

1   Critique the barriers and constraints faced by female entrepreneurs establishing SET ventures.
2   Recognise how stereotypical assumptions surrounding technology can inform a lack of fit between femininity and the SET sector.
3   Analyse the coping strategies adopted by women in order to navigate and negotiate the fraternal culture of SET.

8.3 SCIENCE, ENGINEERING AND TECHNOLOGY ENTERPRISE

Women entrepreneurs are heavily underrepresented in the Science, Engineering and Technology (SET) sector which although associated with high risk ventures, also offers greater potential for fast growth and high returns (Smallbone and Wyer, 2006). It might be assumed that this situation is changing given the increasing numbers of female SET graduates (Mayer, 2006). In fact, evidence from the European Commission (ECDGEI, 2008) indicates that during the early part of the twenty-first century, women have made significant educational advances within the traditionally masculinised field of science, engineering and technology (SET). Indeed, approximately 40 per cent of sector-related Doctoral graduates are now female. However, such educational achievements do not appear to be translated into concomitant career attainment or entrepreneurial activity (Landström, 2007; Wynarczyk, 2009). Whilst women are now gaining the appropriate qualifications and professional accreditation to gain access to the science and technology field, the intrusion of gendered ascriptions can limit their engagement within SET (Crump *et al.*, 2007; Landström, 2007; Marlow and McAdam, 2011). In fact, relatively few will overcome tacit gendered barriers and so, sustain progression within careers or break out into entrepreneurial venturing (Wynarcyzk and Renner, 2006; Holmes, 2007). Drawing from a range of data, Crump *et al.* (2007: 46) found the sector to be overwhelmingly dominated by men such that in all but the lowest levels of data entry work, women constituted less than one-third of the SET workforce.

This underrepresentation of women is often credited to a so-called 'pipeline' effect (Wilson, 2002) which arises from gender-related challenges regarding career progression and so encourages premature exit from related fields of employment. Thus, women are well represented at junior levels but have a diminishing presence in senior positions; this not only affects career development but also, constrains their ability to accrue appropriate entrepreneurial capital (Crump *et al.*, 2007).

8.4 THE PIPELINE EFFECT

In terms of entrepreneurial activity, women currently own approximately just 15 per cent of SET ventures within the European Union (ECDGEI, 2008). Thus, a narrowing 'pipeline' effect constrains women's progression from education to employment and/or entrepreneurship; with their presence within the SET sector defined by early career exits and underrepresentation as innovators and entrepreneurs (Etzkowitz *et al.*, 2000; Wynarczyk, 2009). In addition, it is more difficult to accrue the necessary levels of entrepreneurial capital to support successful new start-ups (Wynarczyk and Renner, 2006). This is perhaps not that surprising as if women are leaving SET careers at relatively early stages in their careers they will struggle to accrue the range of tangible and tacit capitals necessary to establish and grow new ventures. The extant literature would suggest that the source of this pipeline effect is the prevailing normative gendered culture within the SET sector which is steeped within masculinity and so offers a hostile environment for women (Faulkner, 2001; Landström, 2007; Marlow and McAdam, 2011).

So, for those women who do make the transition to SET entrepreneurship, they not only have to weave through the broader gender constraints embedded within the entrepreneurial discourse per se (Ahl, 2006), in addition, they have to negotiate through the masculinised culture of the SET sector. This masculinity manifests in long hours and unbroken employment (Blackwell and Glover, 2008) in addition to competition, individualism and aggression (Wajcman, 1991; Crump et al., 2007). Consequently, many women are excluded from or indeed, exclude themselves from such masculinised career building tactics (Sommerlad and Sanderson, 1998; Wilson, 2002; Bolton and Muzio, 2008). Added to this, are inflexible working patterns which are not conducive to career breaks or part-time unemployment as they are interpreted as portraying 'unseriousness' and thus serve to damage women's credibility and legitimacy as SET professionals (Ranga and Etzkowitz, 2010). Accordingly, the lack of flexibility within such careers is not only instrumental in shaping women's progression but also the consequent gender imbalance at senior levels (Greenfield, 2002; Watts, 2007). The attainment of formal qualifications may lift symbolic barriers and ease women's access to traditionally masculinised careers, but they are unlikely to challenge the embedded gender subordination or undermine gendered barriers to career progression (Holmes, 2007).

8.5 INTERSECTION OF GENDER AND TECHNOLOGY VENTURING

It is widely accepted that the SET sector is not a gender neutral field; rather, masculinity dominates (Faulkner, 2001; Crump et al., 2007). Even when men and women with the same educational attainments are compared, masculine stereotypes associated with SET entrepreneurship can have an adverse effect on female entrepreneurial attentions due to women's lack of affiliation with the masculine traits they perceive to be necessary for SET entrepreneurial activity (Fine, 2010). Consequently, within the masculinised culture of the SET sector, traits which are distinctly male dominate and are 'antithetical to both the stereotyped view of what women are like and stereotype-based norms specifying how they should behave' (Heilman, 2001: 659). A reinforcing set of assumptions genders the image of the typical SET entrepreneur – he is 'male, socially inadequate and isolated' (Crump, 2004: 2). Such stereotypes can serve to reduce women's confidence and interest in entering the sector by alienating them (Wright, 1997). Accordingly, women lack status, visibility and voice within this field.

Although being outnumbered by men in SET is a fact of life for women, as she enters self-employment, her sex will become more salient which can then trigger stereotype threat processes (Fine, 2010). Steele et al. (2002: 385) define a stereotype threat as 'the real time threat of being judged and treated poorly in settings where a negative stereotype about one's group applies'. Moreover, for women who start businesses outside of the 'pink ghettos', they lose an effective protection against stereotype threats – a female role model (Fine, 2010: 56). The lack of critical mass of women within SET results in a lack of female role models, making it

---

BOX 8.1 SPOTLIGHT ON THE WOMEN IN SCIENCE, ENGINEERING AND TECHNOLOGY (WISET)

The Women in Science, Engineering and Technology (WiSET) initiative is located within the in the UK. The main aim driving the initiative is 'to address the under-representation of women in STEM (science, technology, engineering and mathematics)'. The CSE vision is 'Creativity that works', reflecting a passionate belief that by inspiring and capturing the imagination of young people they will be motivated towards science careers and qualifications. But creativity has to work, allowing all young people to reach their highest levels of attainment.

WiSET aims to encourage women and girls into science, engineering, technology and the built environment, to increase rates of recruitment, retention and progression of women to help meet the needs of the economy.

Source: http://www.wiset.org.uk

---

challenging for a woman to imagine herself as a high technology entrepreneur, due to difficulties reconciling the stereotypical image of the high technology entrepreneur (male) with the female identity (Fine, 2010). The stereotypical characterisation of the high technology entrepreneur not only describes how the entrepreneur is (descriptive) but also how they should be (prescriptive) (Gupta *et al.*, 2008). Moreover, if a woman challenges prescriptive stereotypes, this may result in social penalties such as dislike and ostracism (Heliman and Wallen, 2004). Thus, as noted by Etzkowitz *et al.* (2000: 4)

> in many ways, women are unable to choose to do science: as society has largely chosen who will do science through its construction of gender roles whilst from an early age 'boys and girls develop different gendered images of scientists and what they do.

So, the social construction of the SET sector does not reconcile with femininity and serves to construct the message that SET is men's work and thus women do not belong (Trauth, 2002). Furthermore, Cheryan *et al.* (2009) found that women were less interested in computer science as they felt less similar to the typical computer science major; this in turn influenced their sense of belongingness – it was their lack of fit with this stereotypical image that caused disinterest in the discipline.

8.6 FITTING IN WHILST STANDING OUT

As more women attain appropriate qualifications to enter the SET field, they have an increasing presence as researchers, innovators and employees and so, should be generating the capacity to challenge prevailing masculinity. However, often the movement of women into male occupations sometimes results in feminisation of the occupation by speciality (Ridgeway, 1997). Thus, reflecting broader embedded vertical occupational segregation (Holmes, 2007) women are overly represented in lower status work, with a diminishing presence at senior levels, whether in a research, design or managerial capacity (Wilson, 2002; Wynarczyk and Renner, 2006). Furthermore, there is evidence to suggest the existence of feminisation and the emergence of gender roles with women considered to be suited to the softer areas of SET which are considered to require more feminine type attributes such as cooperation, good communication and flexibility; this is in sharp contrast to the more technical jobs which are considered to be more in keeping with the masculine and incidentally lead to senior positions (Panteli et al., 2001; Woodfield, 2002). Consequently, women working within the contemporary technology sector have inherited perceptions of 'what it means to be a woman and how women ought to live and act' (Crotty, 2001: 179) which in this context is articulated as lack of visibility, credibility, status and influence. Accordingly, as Faulkner et al. (2004: 2) note, there is an exceedingly, 'chilly culture for women in the ICT workforce'. The limited presence of women designers, innovators, researchers and/or entrepreneurs has commanded some interest and exploration prompting the development of a feminist critique relating to the prevailing masculinised culture which prevails within the ICT sector (Faulkner, 2001; Walby et al., 2007).

However, efforts have predominantly concentrated on the recruitment of women with the assumption being that once women have acquired critical mass[1] within the SET sectors, advancement and retention would naturally follow (Ranga and Etzkowitz, 2010). Thus, considerably less attention has been afforded to how those who do actually enter this field negotiate their subject positions as women and challenge, accommodate or endure the prevailing culture of masculinity (Marlow and McAdam, 2011). In fact, SET is often constructed a gender neutral and as such individualised agency and meritocracy are dominant features (Kelan, 2009). Despite recognising and identifying situations of discrimination such as fraternity and an old boys' culture, due to a belief in meritocracy, they are reluctant to identify such as gender disadvantage instead choosing to relate to them through individual choice (Panteli et al., 1997; Wajcman, 2004). In fact, the adoption of the honorary man persona (Ogbor, 2000) is one such coping strategy adopted by women within SET to fit in with the masculinity of the sector; with the assumption being that women have to accommodate such masculinity by fitting in (Trauth, 2002). This can manifest in the adoption of particular gestures and dress. In fact, Björkman et al. (1998) note how dress codes are used by women to 'adjust' to male dominated cultures; adopting external trappings of masculinity assists in concealing overt femininity enabling women to blend with the context. Indeed, dress is a critical articulation of gender and particularly so for women who enter masculine fields of work – they need to dissociate from overly feminine

BOX 8.2 CASE STUDY: ANNA HILL – FOUNDING ENTREPRENEUR CEO, SPACE SYNAPSE SYSTEMS LIMITED

Industrial sector

Space/environmental awareness education; Human space interaction design/games industry.

Key motivators

- Using technology for effective communications that pushes the frontiers of participatory multisensorial space experiences.
- Sharing the transformative human experience of space and environment.
- Peaceful and humanitarian use of technology for connecting people across digital divides and diverse geographies and experiences.

Education

BA – Fine Art Sculpture
MA – Fine Art Sculpture

Experience of sector: Space Industry

Worked on an astronaut communications device in the international space industry and developed the concepts and feasibility for an international education and diplomacy communications tool for Space Earth communications.

Opportunity spotting

The human and environmental aspects of the space programme were not being addressed by the dominant culture. There appeared to be a gap between space industry and society, technology and human need. The opportunity for interdisciplinary and more intuitive education emerged. What Space Synapse could offer was creative energy, vision and leadership through collaborative and 'joining the dots'.

Training

No formal business, science or management training so learnt on the job.
My own experience and creative education was my resource.
Good mentorship.

Barriers faced

Space Synapse is a values-driven business existing in a predominantly non-values driven Space industry.

■ Access to finance and investment community.
■ Gaining credibility within a predominately masculine environment.
■ Europe in recession.

Benefits of business ownership

■ In charge of my own destiny.
■ Ability to influence others positively and impart in subtle ways my own life experience and creativity.
■ Purposefulness of innovating original products and services.
■ Challenge of self-development and testing boundaries in myself through taking risks.
■ The interesting, driven and talented people that I have the privilege to work with.

Thanks are due to Anna Hill for writing this case study

dress if they wish to be perceived as gender neutral rather than primarily as sexualised bodies (Alvesson, 1998; McRobbie, 2009). At the same time, women cannot merely adopt normative masculine styles of dress for as Kelan (2009: 174) argues, 'professional women have to perform heterosexual femininity and at the same time have to fulfil the supposedly gender neutral standards of professional work . . . which are, however, saturated with masculinity'. In effect, women are required to carefully self-regulate their subject position to fit normative professional identities without transgressing their ascribed femininity (Marlow and McAdam, 2011). To sum up, women in SET face the same challenges that Ginger Rogers the dancer did when she stated, that she 'did everything Fred Astaire did except backwards and in high heels' (Fine, 2010: 29).

8.7 SUMMARY

Despite the increasing numbers of women undertaking science, computing and information technology qualifications, a narrowing 'pipeline' effect excludes them from senior posts and also, entrepreneurial careers. It has been well documented, particularly within the psychology literature, that such exclusion arises from the lack of 'fit' between ascribed femininity and the cultural ethos that underpins the related fields of science, computing and technology. So, for women who do attain the appropriate qualifications to gain entry into SET, they then need to navigate through an entrenched masculinised culture and in so doing, challenge normative gender roles. However, the coping strategies used to aid such navigation are individualised strategies, as it is assumed that the onus is on the women themselves to change in order to fit into the sector. Therefore, focus should be redirected away from the expectation that women should change in order to accommodate the sector towards challenging the existing masculine cultures and attitudes so deeply entrenched within the sector.

8.8 DISCUSSION POINTS

- 'So Few, So Slow and So Low'. Discuss this statement in relation to women's presence within SET.
- Discuss the impact of the 'pipeline effect' upon women's accrual of entrepreneurial capital.
- Identify some practical solutions that may help to fix the leaky pipeline within SET.

Chapter 9

Empowerment through entrepreneurship

Haya Al-Dajani and Susan Marlow

9.1 INTRODUCTION

This chapter aims to explore the interface of gender, entrepreneuring and context through a critical analysis of empowerment. More specifically, it considers the case of ethnically Palestinian women living in poverty in Amman, Jordan who are operating home-based enterprises within the informal economy. Many of these women engage in craft-based self-employment in order to address their marginal position in society, generate an income and preserve a traditional heritage. The challenges they face, the potential such activities offer for empowerment and emancipation and the implications of this discussion form the basis of this chapter which is structured as follows; first, the notion of empowerment utilising a feminist lens to analyse how this construct interfaces with gender is considered. Second, empirical evidence drawn from a longitudinal study of ethnically Palestinian women living in poverty, using self-employment within the informal economy as an empowerment tool is described. Finally, the implications of the arguments presented are discussed noting that whilst entrepreneuring can have emancipatory and empowering potential, it is not a 'magic' individualised solution to addressing embedded patriarchal systems of disadvantage, but rather, it reinforces Chant's (2008) proposition of a 'feminisation of responsibility and obligation' in overcoming poverty.

9.2 LEARNING OBJECTIVES

On completion of this chapter, students should be able to:

- Understand that entrepreneurial activities are embedded within institutionalised contexts which shape their potential and articulation.
- Critique the Euro–US-centric assumptions underpinning normative analyses of the influence of gender upon entrepreneurship.
- Appreciate that entrepreneurship is unlikely to offer a solution to embedded poverty and female subordination in developing nations.

9.3 ENTREPRENEURING, GENDER AND EMPOWERMENT

In a critical appraisal of the role and position of entrepreneurship in society, Rindova et al., (2009) argue that this construct is far broader than opportunity recognition actioned through venture creation with the objective of wealth generation. Rather, building upon the work of Steyaert (2007), entrepreneurship is reconstructed as entrepreneuring; thus, rather than a noun focused upon outcomes, the construct is re-envisioned as a verb so becomes an active doing. Thus, as 'entrepreneuring', this concept engages with entrepreneurial intentions and outcomes and, in addition, determines how such activities are articulated across and through a range of social, economic, political and institutional landscapes. In this vein, Rindova et al. (2009) draw attention to the emancipatory potential of entrepreneuring; it is not just a productive process but can also be undertaken to address barriers and constraints encountered by individuals in society who in turn act as agents of change. Whilst arguing to broaden the conceptual reach of entrepreneurship theory through their critique, Rindova et al. (2009) do recognise that whilst such activities may offer scope beyond a primarily economic imperative, they are still bounded by institutional limits. Consequently, there is a dynamic iteration between the potential embodied within entrepreneuring and how this can be articulated within the bounds of dominant systems of power and resource limitations and availability. Therefore, women's entrepreneuring could be a reflection of Chant's (2008: 177) 'feminisation of responsibility and obligation' whereby women are 'increasingly in the frontline of dealing with poverty . . . while the social worth of [their] efforts tends to go unacknowledged, robbing them of personal gains, prestige or satisfaction'. This dialogue is embedded within prevailing contexts which additionally enable or constrain the entrepreneuring ambitions of individuals in society (Baughn et al., 2006). As Welter (2011: 165) notes, 'context simultaneously provides individuals with entrepreneurial opportunities and sets boundaries for their actions'. In addition, contextual effects span across the socio-economic environment reflecting culture, institutional norms, time, space and regulation – as such, there are a multiplicity of influences which shape the role and position of entrepreneurial activities (Whetton, 1989). Thus, a critical interface exists between the emancipatory possibilities offered through entrepreneuring activities and the constraints embedded within the contextualised environment.

Focusing specifically upon gender, Welter and Smallbone (2010) evaluate the influence of national and cultural expectations upon women's entrepreneuring in Eastern Europe. It is revealed that prevailing stereotypical expectations regarding feminine weakness and household roles are key barriers women have to navigate to realise entrepreneurial ambitions. Indeed, gender, place and entrepreneurship are critically intertwined at local, national and international levels (Berg, 1997). As such, institutional expectations which position women as primarily domestic actors, act to shape the nature and profile of their enterprises such that their ventures are more likely to be home-based and part-time (Duberley and Carrigan, 2012). This pattern is reflected internationally with differing caveats depending upon women's place within society. Within developed economies, entrepreneurship is deemed as an attractive and desirable option for economic participation whereas, within developing economies and/or those where women experience marginalisation and subordination, it may be the only option they have or conversely, may be denied to them altogether. As such, the manner in which gender is contextually enacted and understood is critical in shaping women's access to entrepreneuring behaviours and in addition, enables or denies their voice and visibility as entrepreneurial actors (Baughn et al., 2006).

Women's empowerment has been widely established in social and economic development research (Meagher, 2010; Sholkamy, 2010; Bordat et al., 2011) and remains a key theme of 'contemporary global political discourse' (McMillan et al., 2011: 189) addressing poverty alleviation, gender inequality and social development (Hiralal, 2010; Kuttab, 2010). Men, who occupy a favoured position in patriarchal contexts, are generally excluded from empowerment research and policy (Molyneux, 2006). The empowerment concept has been applied to poor women in the Global South as they are considered to lack power due to their marginalisation and social exclusion from mainstream society, and the discrimination and gender inequalities they experience (East, 2000; Perrons, 2004; Chant and Pedwell, 2008). While this 'brought a new acceptability, an urgency even, to issues that were once barely countenanced as "development" issues' (Cornwall and Anyidoho, 2010: 146), 'others are troubled by the apparent ease with which an idea that originated in the radical proposition of mobilizing women to transform structural inequalities (Batliwala, 2007) has become so saccharine' (Cornwall and Anyidoho, 2010: 145).

Arising 'contentions and contestations' (Cornwall and Anyidoho, 2010: 144) expressed by feminist critics about women's empowerment theorising and practice (Batliwala, 2007) must not be dismissed. Concerns raised by Batliwala (2007), Cornwall (2007) and Meagher (2010) amongst others agree that 'in contrast to its indigenous notions of empowerment that promised transformation through mobilization and collective action, this alien "empowerment" is individualist, instrumental, neo-liberal. It peddles gender myths that sustain an image of the "good woman" as the deserving object of development assistance' (Cornwall and Anyidoho, 2010: 145). In recognising and accepting these concerns, it is necessary to consider and define women's empowerment as being about process and agency as women themselves must be the significant agents and actors in the process of social change (Mehra, 1997; Al-Dajani and Carter, 2010; Al-Dajani and Marlow, 2010). Indeed, 'unless the intervening processes involve women as agents of that change rather than merely as its recipients, the overall process would not be considered or defined as empowerment' (Malhotra et al., 2002: 7). The importance of agency in the empowerment discourse emerges from 'bottom up' approaches towards development (Narayan *et al.*, 2000). So, rather than a linear process, women's empowerment is a continuous cycle which affects social change (Jabre *et al.*, 1997). This definition reaffirms the individual's role in contributing to social change (Mosedale, 2005) as well as the collective require- ment for achieving it. It also reiterates feminist definitions of empowerment as a journey rather than a destination (Sardenberg, 2008; Eyben and Napier-Moore, 2009; Bordat *et al.*, 2011).

Furthermore, it is recognised that women's entrepreneurial activity has been exploited in neo-liberal agendas to absolve governments of their responsibilities and transfer the onus to individuals to find a solution for their marginalisation and poverty (Narain and Morse, 2008). Thus, according to Chant's (2008) 'feminisa- tion of responsibility and obligation' proposition which suggested that in addition to women's cumbersome responsibility of household/family survival, there is a growing gendered disparity between men's and women's responsibilities for, and contributions to, overcoming poverty across the developing world. She identified three key characteristics of the 'feminisation of responsibility and obligation':

1   *Diversification and intensification of women's inputs to household survival versus stasis or diminution of men's.* This characterisation reflects women's increased engagement in self-employment, 'as well as performing the bulk of unpaid reproductive tasks for husbands, fathers, brothers and sons while men, are not only finding it harder to be the primary economic support for their house- holds but are not increasing their participation in reproductive work either' (Chant, 2008: 178).

2   *Persistent and/or growing disparities in women's and men's capacities to negotiate obligations and entitlements in households.* Here, 'women's mounting responsi- bilities for coping with poverty do not seem to be giving them much leverage in respect of negotiating greater inputs to household survival on the part of men' (Chant, 2008: 179).

3   *Increasing disarticulation between investments/responsibilities and rewards/rights.* Here, 'while responsibilities for dealing with poverty are becoming progres- sively feminised, there seems to be no corresponding increase in women's rights and rewards. Men, on the other hand, despite their lesser inputs, are somehow managing to retain their traditional privileges and prerogatives such as control over income, licence for social freedom and power over household decision making' (Chant, 2008: 182).

To accommodate this critical analysis of empowerment within this chapter, an alternative approach to empowerment using Rindova *et al.*'s (2009) entrepre- neuring as emancipation lens is presented. Through this perspective, poor women's experiences are interpreted and evaluated rather than presenting them as an end in and of themselves. Empowerment offers an analytical frame through which to explore the extent that women utilise entrepreneurship to counter marginalisation and exclusion. Accordingly, analyses of entrepreneuring must feature within current approaches that address and measure empowerment.

9.4 CONTEXT

The critical influence of 'context' on new venture creation and entrepreneuring practices (Welter, 2011), and on women's empowerment (Cornwall and Anyidoho, 2010) is well recognised. Accordingly, specific socio-economic, political, market and institutional contexts are key to fostering, enabling and enacting entrepreneurial activity (Aldrich, 2000; Locke, 2000; Shane et al., 2003; Welter, 2011). Consequently, this analysis is transposed to explore the contextualised entrepreneurial experiences of ethnically Palestinian women living in poverty and operating within the informal economy of the Arab developing economy of Jordan.

As the Arab Spring slides into what Goulding (2011) suggested could be a 'Feminist Fall', the Arab Middle East continues to be characterised by social uprisings and political instability, speculation about future ownership of its boundless energy resources, and the overriding impression of a homogeneous people with a common culture (van Doorn-Harder, 2011) initiating the next stage in its long and complex history. What is masked by this image, and rarely discussed, is an unsettled reality of long-term, multi-generational displacement (IRiN, 2011) that is shared by millions who live as refugees or displaced persons in the wider Middle East. The sixtieth anniversary of the Palestinian 'Nakbeh' was marked in 2008; this Arabic word means catastrophe; its use usually refers to 1948 when the state of Israel was created on Palestinian land, forcing hundreds of thousands of Palestinians into exile (Kuttab, 2008). Sixty-four years on, there are more Palestinians living in the Diaspora than within the Palestinian territories (Merriman, 2007). Jordan hosts the largest number of ethnic Palestinians residing outside the Palestinian Territories – approximately three million individuals (Khawaja and Tiltnes, 2002), comprising about two-thirds of the total population (CIA, 2009). This influx has led to socio-political tensions such that integration and economic stability remain top priorities for successive political regimes within Jordan (Fanek, 2005; Tabbaa, 2010), and continue to challenge existing policies regarding nationality and citizenship, settlement, and right of return, especially in light of the Arab Spring that has engulfed the region since the beginning of 2011. The Arab Spring has contributed to furthering the social exclusion of such marginalised groups. By focusing on unifying mainstream populations, both reformists and the political establishments have contributed to push the agendas of the region's long-term displaced even further into the margins. In particular, poorer women in these populations who are already confined within the boundaries of their homes have become increasingly invisible, since they are already socially, economically and politically excluded from the mainstream in their host societies.

Labels including 'refugees', 'displaced community', 'diasporic' and 'migrants' have all inaccurately been associated with the ethnic Palestinian community residing outside the Palestinian Territories and within the Middle East region. This is due to the fact that some Palestinians continue to be refugees, others displaced and many consider themselves diasporic. However, no label reflects the ethnic Palestinians who have become nationals and citizens of countries such as Jordan, and none of these Palestinians would contemplate the label of migrant which denotes voluntary relocation. Given the complexity and diversity associated with the Palestinian socio-political identity and status in the Middle East region, the term 'ethnic Palestinian' to encompass the Palestinians living in Jordan as Jordanian nationals of Palestinian origin, refugees or displaced persons is adopted. The term minority is not utilised in this study since the ethnic Palestinian community constitutes two-thirds of the Jordanian population (CIA, 2009).

In a region where ethnic identities are deliberately concealed to maintain social harmony, the entrepreneurial experiences of women belonging to diverse ethnic groups either get absorbed and included within the dominant group, or remain excluded and largely invisible. Examples of this include BADIL (2002), CAW-TAR (2007) and Charrad (2011). Thus, a discussion of ethnic minorities and women's entrepreneuring has yet to emerge from the Middle East region. By acknowledging the ethnic Palestinian poor women's entrepreneuring and the extent to which it contributes to the local and national Jordanian economy, this chapter introduces a further dimension regarding ethnic women's entrepreneuring and empowerment in developing economies. This contributes to the increasing interest and research documentation on Arab women's engagement in self-employment and entrepreneurship (IFC-GEM, 2006; Weeks, 2009) which recognises that women's experiences of entrepreneuring within the Middle East region have been neglected by researchers and policy makers (Al-Dajani and Carter, 2010; Al-Dajani and Marlow, 2010). This has further exacerbated women's invisibility within the region's economic and development strategies which recognise that women's economic participation in the Arab Middle East region remains the world's lowest at 26 per cent compared with the world average of 55.6 per cent (World Bank, 2010; Weeks, 2009). Such figures however do not account for women's economic activity within the informal sector as local and international policy makers continue to ignore the contributions this makes to national economies (Al-Budirate, 2009). A feminised focus upon women's experiences as entrepreneurs and agents of change in this context is therefore, essential for gaining a clearer analytical understanding of women's entrepreneuring in this region.

9.5 DATA COLLECTION

Given that women's empowerment is a process which can only be assessed upon a temporal basis, a longitudinal qualitative research approach was adopted.

Accordingly, the study spanned a ten-year period, constituting three consecutive phases of data collection in Amman, Jordan from 1999 to 2009. The participants were forty-three ethnic Palestinian poor women operating traditional embroidery home-based enterprises within the informal economy. They were initially identified via eight organisations operating within the formal economy that subcontracted work from the home-based entrepreneurs. Through initial semi-structured interviews lasting up to three hours, and follow-up interviews and/or telephone conversations undertaken at regular intervals within the study period, how the participants negotiated, interpreted and addressed the realities which confronted them on a daily basis with regards to social exclusion, marginality and patriarchal subjection was explored. This adheres to Steyaert and Katz's (2004) 'everydayness of entrepreneurship'. The qualitative analysis was undertaken manually, as NVivo remains unreliable when used in Arabic (QSR, 2008). The themes drawn from the data reduction of the interview material informed three critical constructs: contextualised entrepreneurial motivations, women's entrepreneuring and empowerment outcomes.

9.6 THE SAMPLE

The selection of participants was driven by a conceptual question that linked empowerment, gender, ethnicity and entrepreneurship. Purposive sampling was adopted to ensure that the participants reflected the characteristics of the study in that they were all home-based female producers making and selling high quality traditional craft work. Generally, the participants and their home-based enterprises reflected the characteristics of the population in terms of age, ethnicity, educational attainment, displacement status and home-based enterprise characteristics. Thus, the overall sample was:

1   Married or divorced and aged 16 or above as this is the legal age for marriage in Jordan (UNIFEM, 2004).
2   Engaged in home-based enterprise whereby all self-employed activities took place within the home.
3   Operated home-based enterprises for a minimum of two years (at the beginning of the study in 1999) located in the East Amman region.

Table 9.1 outlines participant education levels and number of years as home-based entrepreneurs operating within the traditional embroidery sector. The majority had completed secondary schooling; three participants (7 per cent) were divorced reflecting the low divorce rate overall within Jordan (UNIFEM, 2004). The mean age of the participants was 45; the average age of the home-based enterprise was 26 years with the oldest home-based enterprise being 50 years old and the youngest 12 years old. Such figures indicate long-term sustainability. All participants are given pseudonyms to protect their identities.

Table 9.1 Demographic data of the participants from 2009

Participant	Age	Education level	No. of children	Declared monthly income from one subcontractor (UK £)	Years as home-based producer
Adila	31	Secondary	1	52	16
Alia	31	Secondary	1	50	15
Bahija	33	Secondary	2	40	14
Basma	34	Primary	3	63	20
Dalal	57	Primary	5	300	40
Dana	38	Primary	6	62	24
Fathiya	47	Secondary	3	125	30
Fatima	50	Secondary	3	55	15
Firyal	58	Primary	6	70	42
Ghalia	36	Secondary	3	80	16
Hana	40	Secondary	1	40	21
Hiba	46	Primary	6	53	32
Hidaya	32	Secondary	2	75	16
Huda	37	Secondary	4	52	16
Iman	57	Primary	5	65	42
Jalila+	46	Secondary	1	68	30
Juhaina	53	Primary	4	68	30
Khadija	66	Primary	8	90	34
Laila	63	Primary	5	75	50
Lamis	38	Secondary	3	68	22
Lubna+	33	Primary	2	68	21
Madiha	35	Secondary	3	57	18
Maha	64	Primary	7	85	40
Majida	32	Secondary	1	64	17
Manal	49	Secondary	5	69	20
Maryam	28	Secondary	1	40	12
Maysa	41	Secondary	4	130	20
Muna+	44	Secondary	3	60	30
Nafisa	39	Secondary	2	70	23
Nihal	49	Primary	6	73	28
Noura	36	Secondary	1	60	20
Nur	39	Secondary	3	250	21
Omaima	53	Primary	1	80	37
Rajha	48	Primary	5	70	28

(Continued)

Table 9.1 *(Continued)*

Participant	Age	Education level	No. of children	Declared monthly income from one subcontractor (UK £)	Years as home-based producer
Rana	44	Secondary	1	65	24
Rawan	56	Secondary	4	150	36
Riham	38	Secondary	4	190	17
Sadeer	51	University	4	130	33
Samiha	59	Secondary	5	110	40
Sara	42	Secondary	3	70	25
Suha	55	Secondary	3	100	35
Sundos	47	Primary	4	70	25
Um	66	Secondary	3	380	50

9.7 THE EMPIRICAL EVIDENCE

Analyses of female entrepreneurship, empowerment and social capital have inaccurately assumed homogeneity of background and context; such normative modelling effectively excludes the migrant, ethnic minority, refugee and displaced women residing in a developing host economy (see for example, Katungi *et al.*, 2008). However, given the limited socio-political and employment rights afforded to such groups in their developing host countries, home-based entrepreneuring within the informal economy provides one of the very few options available for income generation and social engagement (Granovetter, 1985; Bordat *et al.*, 2011). Consequently, analysing the intersectionality of women's place, empowerment and contextualised entrepreneuring is critical to enriching entrepreneurship research.

Similar to other regions in the developing world, women-owned home-based enterprises operating within the informal economy in Jordan reflect the traditionally feminised production of traditional and sometimes, indigenous craft goods. Such small-scale units can develop the necessary skills and styles to produce such products (Chifos, 2007). Analyses addressing traditional craft production and its impact on gender and socio-cultural norms have assumed that such activity is undertaken by indigenous women, residing and operating within their home countries (Jena, 2007), or as members of established ethnic minorities in Europe and the United States (Buller, 2007). To this extent, the gendered production of traditional craft has been criticised for reproducing a gendered division of labour, gender inequalities and limited development and empowerment for women (Vallianatos and Raine, 2007). However, this critique does not acknowledge that

87

traditional craft production is often the only link between displaced women and their lost heritage, culture and identity (Ramussen, 2005). Hence, their traditional craft production contributes positively to the development of their social identity, heightened socio-political awareness (Al-Dajani and Marlow, 2010) and enterprising activity (Al-Dajani and Carter, 2010; Al-Dajani and Marlow, 2010). As such, traditional craft enterprise is intersected with women's empowerment which leads to a growing sense of power and control over domestic and community resources (Al-Dajani, 2007).

The longitudinal approach utilised in this study facilitated the tracking of participant entrepreneurial motives over the ten-year period. At the beginning of the study in 1999, all participants agreed that home-based enterprise was their only option in order to combine family responsibilities and demands with income generation. They also agreed that their primary motive for establishing their enterprises was to maintain the traditional Palestinian art of embroidery which symbolised their heritage. Thus, Queen Rania's[1] adoption of traditionally embroidered dresses for various public and official events since her coronation in 1999 was a critical royal endorsement for the sector. Ten years after the coronation, Queen Rania's appearance on the front covers of international magazines such as *Hello!* in June 2009 indicated her continued role as a global icon whose trends are followed by many throughout Jordan, the Middle East and beyond. All participants acknowledged the positive influence this had on their sector. Despite the extent of political turmoil in the region between 1999 and 2009, and the effects of the global economic recession on Jordan in 2009, overall, the traditional embroidery sector continued to be profitable. All participants were subcontracted by established Jordanian organisations operating within the formal economy and whose customers were predominantly local or regional, affluent and fashion conscious women. In 2009, the majority of participants agreed with Hana that 'everyone wants dresses like the Queen's and that's very good for us . . . we love to make them although they are very demanding but it is our bread and butter'. This was echoed by Bahija, whose products were sold in Canada when in 2009 she said 'I have never been to Canada, but there everyone knows Queen Rania and they want to support the women in Jordan. That's why they buy my creations . . . I make sure my work is top quality so it really looks like Rania's dresses and then, they will want more from me'.

Given the close associations with their history, tradition and displacement, the women's shared motive over the course of the ten-year study, was intensified by the majority of participants especially during periods of increased political tensions in the region; to maintain the Palestinian identity and heritage through their embroidery enterprises. The combination of the traditional embroidery revival motivation and the impact of royal endorsement, plus the entrepreneurs' political awareness and engagement, and their entrepreneurial motives for preserving the Palestinian identity contributed to the empowerment of the home-based displaced embroiderers. These themes, together with enterprise sustainability, have led to the emergence of several opportunities.

9.8 ENTREPRENEURING OPPORTUNITIES

Of great importance to the participants was the mission to keep the Palestinian heritage and identity alive through their traditional embroidery enterprises. Furthermore, they expressed concern about their livelihoods defined by deprivation and social exclusion within the disadvantaged neighbourhoods of East Amman. Promoting a sense of artistry and creativity with a Palestinian identity was difficult when globally this identity was synonymous with violence, terrorism and extremism. This notion of identity was further exacerbated by their personal struggles in defining their varied sub-identities and multiple roles as entrepreneurs, displaced women, mothers, wives and Palestinians.

The evident political engagement of these women is embedded within their own life histories and widely shared amongst their communities. In a socio-politically volatile region, they have managed to engage their political awareness and experienced marginalisation with their entrepreneurial drive. For example, the eight participants aged 46 and over, became involved in their mothers' home-based enterprises from the age of six. Sundos recalled growing up in Amman's refugee camps following the 1967 war with Israel, and in 1999 stated 'we attended to essential tasks but not the embroidery itself . . . I had to go to the shops outside the camp to buy threads and needles, go to other embroiderers on the camp to collect products for my mother, and I also collected our family's rations from UNRWA'.

Other evidence of political engagement lies in the women's enterprising embroidery whereby they made specific products to aid the region's victims of war, displacement and/or political tensions, and to create social awareness amongst clientele. A significant number of participants engaged in legitimate awareness creating activities about the Palestinian intifada between 2002 and 2004 by making embroidered scarves marking the uprising and sold through local SMEs and NGOs located within the formal economy to raise funds to support the victims. Similarly, in 2009, the majority of participants created further traditionally embroidered products to be sold through the same formal economy organisations engaged in lawful fund raising activities to support the victims of the Israeli offensive on Gaza. Furthermore, when the overall sector chose to mourn the victims of the terrorist attacks on Amman in 2005 by closing their businesses for three to seven days, the displaced women entrepreneurs delivered a very clear message on the extent to which they are connected with the mainstream population and unsympathetic to the bombers. Maha in 2009 recalled that 'we are always considered to be the bad guys, the terrorists, but we're not, if anything, we are always the victim . . . we were so shocked by the bombs here and we were so scared too. I pray nothing like that ever happens again here'.

When reflecting on her socio-political role in 2009, Nur – a 39-year old owner of a 21-year-old home-based enterprise – gave a very astute analysis stating that 'the buyers of all these products feel very good when they make their purchase because they think they are helping the people of Palestine, Iraq or somewhere else, but they don't realise that they are also helping us, we are not on their mind'. The results from this study indicate the participants' political awareness and engagement which they channelled into creative, innovative and socially responsible activity which led to several outcomes; economic contributions channelled to those excluded from mainstream society, increased mainstream social awareness about the plights of these peoples and finally, a positive socio-economic influence on their own enterprises' business activity. From another angle, these results show that while the controlling authorities banned all political protest activities, they assume the traditional patriarchal model whereby women are political followers and men political leaders. In fact, these women were highly engaged with political activism but remained invisible to the authorities in sharp contrast to the surveillance afforded to male activists.

These results illustrate how the women's political awareness, entrepreneuring and empowerment are cyclically entwined whereby the political awareness as a motivational drive and passion engages the women in a traditional embroidery home-based enterprise and through this engagement, the women gain increased control as they gain access to resources, enhance their socio-political awareness, participate through selective channels to address their concerns and gain control as they manipulate their imposed invisibility and silence, to achieve chosen goals.

9.9 EMPOWERMENT INDICATORS

In analysing the participant entrepreneurs' home-based enterprise development from start-up to current establishment and the effects this had on their empowerment process, some trends reveal an overlap between entrepreneuring and empowerment. All participants reflected on their frustration and awareness of the persistent socio-political inequalities between men and women within their displaced group, and the marginalisation of their overall displaced group, as motivations for operating home-based enterprises within this sector. This demonstrates a strong understanding and consciousness whereby the participants are aware and knowledgeable regarding the socio-political circumstances governing their realities. Evidently, by choosing to establish home-based enterprises focused on the production of traditional embroidery, the participants proactively contributed to:

■ Creating increased awareness about the heritage of their ethnic group.
■ Reviving their lost heritage.

- A profitable and sustainable sector within the region's volatile environment.
- Elevating their individual social status within their immediate communities and sometimes, beyond them.
- The creation of outlets for non-threatening forms of socio-political protest.

While this illustrates Chant's (2008) 'feminisation of responsibility and obligation', it also reflects the notion of Rindova *et al.*'s (2009) emancipatory entrepreneuring. In effect, entrepreneurial activity in this context is a socio-economic/political endeavour. Whilst there is little dispute that these women use home-based enterprise to address material poverty, this is not the only outcome of their entrepreneuring behaviours. In addition, there is a clearly articulated political agenda whereby the fine craft goods produced are symbolic of a specific culture and heritage threatened by displacement and exile. Moreover, embroidered goods were used more directly as an articulation of specific political protest. Regarding the relationship between patriarchal subordination and entrepreneuring, the evidence suggests that the degree to which these women can challenge embedded disadvantage varies according to individual situation. Thus, for some women, their enterprises were celebrated within the family and community where the economic benefits were fully appreciated resulting in enhanced personal status. Yet, other women were not able to reveal the full nature and extent of their activities as it was deemed unacceptable. Consequently, there is an uncertain and fragmented form of emancipation here; whilst there can be little doubt as to the socio-political facet of entrepreneuring in this context, it was however not axiomatically available to all women within the community.

Thus, the interactive process of empowerment through entrepreneuring is focused on making decisions and achieving control, attaining creative control over the creation of their products and gaining independent market access were consistently frustrating and problematic for some participants over the course of the ten-year study. The few who did report creative control and market access tended to be older in age and with extensive experience beyond twenty years in this saturated sector. They had an established reputation for quality as Samiha expressed in 2009, 'we continue to instil our souls into the embroidery we produce', and held leadership status amongst the producers within the sector and its clients.

The majority of participants with market access, but limited creative control, claimed that such constraints were influenced by the client. This negatively impacted upon their non-economic outcomes of empowerment such as 'making decisions and having choices', 'leadership' and 'self identity'. They shared Maysa's anxiety when she stated in 2005 that 'her [the client] expectation is that the embroidery should be PERFECT, and I know I can do it without any problems . . . but I don't sleep at night worrying if she'll like it or not . . . she's been my client for eight years and still, I feel the same nervousness every time she comes to collect an item'.

91

One further small subgroup within the sample claimed that they were limited to predominantly one large subcontracting agency and their creative control was largely determined by the contractor. Firyal's statement explaining the reason for this in 2005 was echoed by the majority within this small subgroup, 'I don't want to create extra work for myself . . . it is much easier if they tell me exactly what they want done, and how to do it, and then I give it to them as they want it . . . why should I create more work for myself and then they reject it anyway or it doesn't sell?' This statement illustrates that Firyal and her counterparts made a decision by deliberately choosing to limit their embroidery control and market access and to this extent, demonstrate non-economic empowerment outcomes. While they shared the initial entrepreneurial motivations with the entrepreneurs with market access and creative control, their future motivations resulting from their empowerment outcomes may differ to the extent that this group exhibited more risk aversion than the former group.

9.10 SUSTAINABILITY OF THE HOME-BASED ENTERPRISE

Given the volatile socio-political nature of the Middle East region, the survival and long-term sustainability of women-owned home-based enterprises can be unpredictable. However, while all participating enterprises were evidently sustainable in the long term and expected to continue successfully after the global economic recession and the Arab Spring, all participants reported the extent to which their business activity grew or contracted depending on the socio-political climate of the region. Within this region, a crisis in one area can lead to an opportunity in another. Within the study's ten-year period, there were regular unexpected significant business increases in the traditional embroidery sector in Jordan when political crises escalated elsewhere in the region, for example, during and following the Israel–Lebanon war in 2006. Not only did tourist numbers increase dramatically in Jordan as a result of this war, but also regional businesses who were engaged with Lebanese partners arrived in Amman looking for alternative partners specialising within the traditional embroidery sector. For the participants, this balanced the negative effects on their enterprises when tourism decreased dramatically and Jordan's socio-political stability was distorted following: the 9/11 New York bombings in 2001; the start of the war on Iraq in 2003; and the terrorist attacks on Amman in 2005. Added to the participants' ethnic status and their informal sector home-based enterprises, these circumstances and the arising volatility may contribute to the participants' preference for long-term sustainability and growth aversion. The findings from this study suggest that all participants operated long-term sustainable enterprises with growth potential. However, the growth constraint resulted from the entrepreneurs' growth aversion, which was heavily influenced by the specific socio-cultural and political context of marginalisation in which they operated.

9.11 SUMMARY

When discussing the implications of the arguments presented within this chapter, it is noted that whilst entrepreneuring can have emancipatory and empowering potential, it is not a 'magic' individualised solution to addressing embedded patriarchal systems of disadvantage thus, reconsidering Chant's (2008) proposition of the feminisation of responsibility and obligation, the results confirm her proposition. In this case, the government marginalise the rights and voices of those who are not citizens; in addition, by definition, the informal economy is not recognised or acknowledged. Therefore, the women in this study were denied a subject position as citizens or entrepreneurs and so, were doubly ignored. If the feminisation of responsibility and obligation enhances empowerment, and upgrades women's socio-political status within their immediate environments, this should be positive at the individual level. However, it is recognised that this is insufficient for culturally aware and recognised gender equality. More collective action is required to improve women's status within patriarchal societies and so challenge embedded subordination. Clearly, social change has to begin somewhere; when at the grassroots level as in the case here, this illustrates independence and ownership. If entrepreneuring enhances this, then it's a good thing! Top-down approaches and policies are not an ideal solution on their own as they do not account for micro systems and localised contexts. As such, policy intervention should be an iterative process informed and guided by expert insight which also recognises and accounts for local needs; in the absence of dialogue, top-down policy is likely to be deemed as unwelcome interference.

9.12 DISCUSSION POINTS

- To what extent can entrepreneuring be considered emancipatory and empowering for women living in poverty in developing nations?
- This chapter presented evidence from women operating within the traditional craft sector. List three other sectors in which women operate home-based enterprises within the informal economy in developing countries. Discuss the relevance of the 'empowerment through entrepreneurship' argument to self-employed women operating in these other sectors.
- Given the critical discussion in this chapter, what role should (a) government, and (b) international agencies, play in improving the lives of poor women in developing countries? Explain and justify your answer.

Chapter 10

Conclusion: setting research agendas

Susan Marlow

10.1 INTRODUCTION

As is evident from the wealth of material presented within this text, exploring and analysing the relationship between entrepreneuring intentions, behaviours, ambitions and gender encompasses an extremely diverse range of multi-disciplinary issues. One of the first commentaries upon this relationship emerged with the work of Schwartz in 1976 with her recognition that gender intersects with, and influences experiences of, entrepreneuring. Yet, the discrete field of female entrepreneurship did not emerge as a coherent and continuous strand of research until a decade later (Carter and Shaw, 2006). Since the early 1990s, it is fair to suggest that this body of work has grown from a mere trickle to a veritable flood such that for example, in a recent literature review, Neergaard *et al.* (2011) identify more than 700 related academic papers. This does not account for popular and grey literatures which considerably swells this coverage (Carter and Shaw, 2006; Radu and Redien-Collot, 2008). Thus, it is fair to say that the *female* entrepreneur has arrived as a topic of research, a subject of policy generation and a separate practitioner category. Indeed, this is very evident within this text which ranges over issues from theoretical relationships between the constructs of gender and entrepreneurship to more empirical work on how entrepreneuring might act as an empowering change agent for women.

Naturally, in any developing discourse there are complementary and contrasting strands and in addition, gaps which demand further exploration. This text has explored a number of key issues in current debate but can only offer a selective analysis, thus we conclude the discussion with suggestions for areas of future research. To construct any meaningful or convincing strategy about how research might usefully develop in the future, it is essential to develop a brief overview of the themes which have dominated the literature in the past. From this assessment, we can offer informed speculation regarding fruitful future pathways. Accordingly, this chapter has a simple structure – a comment upon key advances since the 1990s followed by a more nuanced consideration of future possibilities and finally, concluding comments which assess the place and importance of the gender debate within the entrepreneurial discourse.

10.2 PAST THEMES AND CONCERNS

One critical aspect which does emerge in generating this discussion is a shift in terminology applied to this particular field. Thus, until fairly recently, the focus has been almost exclusively upon women's experiences of business ownership generally articulated as explorations of 'female' entrepreneurship. Consequently, the unit of analysis has been the woman herself and how she approaches, manages and engages with the field of entrepreneurship which has been represented as a neutral activity available and accessible to all. In taking this ontological stance, early research efforts largely placed women as an interloper in the field who demonstrated a relatively poor fit with established incumbents – men (Carter and Shaw, 2006). Reflecting this ontology, epistemological framing uncritically used gender as a variable whereby the entrepreneurial activities of men and women were compared across a range of performance indicators with women inevitably positioned in deficit such that their enterprises were condemned as smaller, weaker, lacking growth orientation, home-based, part-time; indeed, almost every detrimental business term possible was visited upon the hapless female entrepreneur (Marlow et al., 2009). This in turn promoted a range of policy interventions across developed economies which reflected a similar message, namely, how to 'fix' the problem of the female entrepreneur (Small Business Service, 2003). To quote more recent work by Taylor and Marlow (2009: 1), the underpinning subtext rested upon the regretful notion of 'why can't a woman be more like a man?' and relatedly, 'what can be done to make this happen?'. Indeed, the liberal feminist agenda (Calás et al., 2009) was a largely unrecognised and uncritically acknowledged conceptual frame for the whole debate with just a few dissenting voices such as Mirchandani (1999) and Marlow (2002). A key problem with the tone of this discussion was revealed in the early 2000s with seminal work by Ogbor (2000) and Ahl (2004). Ogbor raised a broad critique of the entrepreneurial field and particularly, the failure of prevailing literature to recognise the institutional biases embedded within the discourse in which ascribed characteristics such as race, class and gender inherently shape how entrepreneurship is accessed, understood and enacted. Ahl (2004, 2006) developed a poststructural feminist critique which questioned the alleged gender neutrality of the entrepreneurial discourse. Rather, she argued that entrepreneurship is embedded in masculinity; the textual representation of the entrepreneur is inevitably male, which, in turn, positions women as outsiders or intruders to this field. However, as Ahl points out, much of the extant literature drawn from the 'gender as a variable' approach actually failed to find many significant differences between men and women firm owners. Yet, given embedded gendered assumptions, the quest for difference persisted (and persists) with small variations exaggerated to satisfy social expectations of male dominance and female deficit.

The body of work which emerged at the turn of the twenty-first century that began to question the female deficit thesis centred upon female entrepreneurship but also marked the beginnings of greater conceptual plurality with more nuanced analyses of the influence of gender upon entrepreneuring. Thus, this analytical shift marked greater engagement with theoretical criticism rather than the previous focus upon descriptive comment. However, it is worthy of note that for the most part, reflecting broader debates such as those within Critical Management Studies, gender is a proxy for femininity (Ashcraft, 2011). Indeed, as Kelan (2009: 166) remarks, gender 'sticks' to women in a very specific and indeed, gendered manner supporting the notion that masculinity is the default so needs no explanation or rational defence. As a more theoretically informed debate has emerged in the 2000s regarding the nexus between gender and entrepreneuring, the problem of causality has also been considered regarding to what extent gender as a variable can be effectively identified as a definitive influence upon entrepreneuring (Gill, 2011). This debate introduces notions of intersectionality which suggests that previous work has been embedded in generic racist and heteronormative assumptions that uncritically positions gender subordination as universal and dominant within the hierarchy of disadvantageous social ascriptions. Consequently, gender theorising within entrepreneurship is in danger of emerging, at best, as a blunt instrument which assumes that gender only applies to women and homogenises disadvantage whilst at worst, in making such assumptions reproduces the subordination it purports to critique.

Whilst it is apparent that the shifting analytical tone of the literature now recognises that broader socio-economic gender disadvantages critically shape women's approach to and experience of entrepreneuring, this has not been accommodated within policy interventions. For the most part, the notion of women needing 'fixing' persists with separate spaces, courses and activities offered which presume that their entry to entrepreneurship originates from a fundamentally different stance from that of men. This perpetuates and embeds the notion of difference and deficit which requires assistance; moreover, it conflates agency and structure. As such, the underpinning assumption suggests that, within the entrepreneurial context, institutional structures which bound gendered systems can be challenged and undermined by personal individualised agency. This is unlikely; rather once again, individual women are tasked with taking responsibility for and finding solutions to systematic institutional socio-economic gendered bias. Accordingly, the argument here is not to deny gender disadvantage as a delimiting factor to female potential but rather, to position women as responsible for addressing their own subordination.

Consequently, to progress debate a nuanced and theoretically informed critique is now essential to strengthen analytical understanding of the relationship between gender and entrepreneuring and that in addition, recognises the intersectional nature of this debate. Furthermore, given the reach of entrepreneurship as a policy and practitioner issue, new pathways have to be forged to ensure theoretical advances act as a critique to broader assumptions and activities. How this might be address through future research avenues is now considered.

10.3 MOVING FORWARD – POTENTIAL RESEARCH OPPORTUNITIES AND PATHWAYS

In drawing up suggestions for future developments, it is helpful to think of the field as framed within the broad generic construct of gender but, acknowledging critiques raised above, has diverse articulations. Indeed, a pertinent critique of the current approach relates to the overly descriptive, universal use of key constructs, so the first point regarding future trends is the fundamental need to move on from assumptions of homogeneity fuelled solely by a shared biology. In recognising that it is gender rather than sex which constructs experiences of entrepreneuring, it is axiomatic that critical analyses of the contextualised, diverse and nuanced manner in which this notion is reproduced must sit at the heart of future work. Accordingly, in outlining some possibilities for future avenues, we have divided these observations and suggestions into discrete sections which of course, will have overlapping themes but hopefully, also indicate distinct gaps where value can be added to contemporary debate. To commence, we develop a critique of current theorising which draws upon several strands of analytical thought as only by progressing the conceptual framing of debate can more substantive issues be meaningfully contextualised. Having considered theoretical progression, a small number of substantive areas are discussed but these are by no means exhaustive but rather, possibilities and examples. If it is agreed that there is scope for both theoretical and empirical development in the field then quite clearly, some attention to method and methodology is necessary. Finally, we conclude with a short general observation regarding the broader possibilities represented through the exploration of gender and entrepreneurship for the entrepreneurial field per se.

10.4 THEORETICAL GENDER AND ENTREPRENEURSHIP

As has been argued (Neergaard et al., 2011), explorations of the relationship between gender and entrepreneurship have tended towards description, depended upon small self-reported samples with little evidence of theoretical advancement. To remedy this lacuna, future work must be embedded within clear conceptual foundations. So, for example, drawing upon the broad and complex field of feminist theory to move beyond merely describing the detrimental influence of gender upon women's entrepreneuring is essential to develop explanatory

97

frameworks. Given the diverse range of perspectives covered by the umbrella of feminist theorising there is much scope here for advancement. In addition, critically evaluating the overdependence upon liberal feminism, as a default assumption underpinning most current theorising and policy formation, is essential to reveal a narrow and bounded epistemology. Indeed, it is difficult to consider how understanding can progress without stronger theorising informing research outcomes. In addition to developing stronger feminist critiques of the association between gender and entrepreneuring, other competing theoretical frameworks can be usefully employed to develop debate particularly regarding the scope for emancipation and empowerment. The agentic potential within entrepreneurship to generate an 'enterprising self' capable of managing and promoting an individual biography has been acknowledged as a critical constituent of the contemporary neo-liberal project (Beck, 1992; Du Gay, 2002; Ogbor, 2000; McRobbie, 2009) but how this amalgam of constructs promotes gender bias requires further attention. The emergence of neo-liberalism and the enterprise of the self are clearly complementary to and indeed, fuel the contemporary entrepreneurial project. The notion of the individually created biography is not only central to the entrepreneurial debate but also to that of postfeminism (Genz and Brabon, 2010). Postfeminism inspires much debate regarding its form and capacity as a critical reflection upon women's role and place in society; it is not our purpose to discuss that here. However, a key tenet of postfeminism focuses upon the capacity of contemporary women to utilise their agentic power to create a preferred subject position so, becoming entrepreneurs of the self (du Gay, 2002). It is acknowledged that the research agenda in entrepreneurship and gender studies is reaching into theoretical engagement with the conditions under which the constructed subject of the entrepreneurial self is available to women. Yet, positioning this debate to intersect with the postfeminist critique would develop greater conceptual clarity regarding the broader socio-economic and political implications of assumptions of accessibility and neutrality surrounding entrepreneurship. Accordingly, whilst there is growing recognition of the importance of the need to critically evaluate the potential offered by entrepreneurship as emancipation, how gender might shape such potential requires further critical evaluation.

Further opportunities to challenge narrow theoretical constraints lie within critiques of the association between gender, women and entrepreneuring. As noted above, there is a normative assumption that gender refers to femininity and within the context of entrepreneuring, this is narrowed down to women's business ownership. This narrow and limiting assumption effectively renders both the performance of masculinity and how men challenge or reproduce such performances invisible and unexplored. Indeed, as the default position in this debate, masculinity loses a tangible identity and is not considered a 'doing' but just something that 'is'. In effect, the gendered position of those who constitute the majority population within entrepreneurship has been rendered invisible. So, we have not questioned to what extent most self-employed men identify with the masculinised stereotypical entrepreneurial role which is seamlessly attached to them by virtue of gender. Accordingly, recognising and unpicking articulations of masculinity and its generic application warrant discrete analyses and conceptual critique. Indeed, questioning how the masculinity subtext within the field is articulated may be the first step to revealing the rather more mundane and ordinary nature of entrepreneurship. In so doing, a further contribution to gender studies may emerge as we illuminate the constructed entrepreneurial discourse as a masculine chimera to which the female must aspire, is condemned for never reaching but, in essence, this is a goal which does not and never will exist. In effect, gendered constructs within entrepreneurship are subordinating forces with analytical substance but no associated empirical characterisation. Thus, in addition to developing more sophisticated epistemological approaches to illuminating the interface between entrepreneuring and gender, there is clearly space for critical realism to contribute to debate.

To conclude thoughts on the future of gender theorising in the entrepreneurial context, we have critiqued the axiomatic acceptance of a unitary gender analysis (focus upon women/femininity) suggesting this needs to encompass the binary stance (feminism/masculinism; men/women) but this does not recognise the queer agenda. Whilst there is some work in the entrepreneurial field which explores gay entrepreneurship (Galloway, 2011) this has not been developed as a sophisticated contribution to queer studies. Accordingly, the manner in which heteronormativity dominates and more so, that it is uncritically accepted as a normative stance is both remarkable and profoundly depressing as a symbol of the narrow and bounded understanding and reach of entrepreneurship.

10.5 INTERSECTIONALITY

As has been suggested above, one profitable avenue for future research lies within clearer recognition of not only gendered heterogeneity to moving away from generic presumptions but also in stronger critiques of how gender intersects with other social ascriptions. Within the broader feminist debate, the intersection of gender with race, class, sexuality et cetera is an established and much discussed aspect (Bowden and Mummery, 2009). Indeed, those such as bell hooks have developed powerful critiques of the middle class racist assumptions which have normatively informed both first and second wave feminist argument (hooks, 1981). Accordingly, contemporary discussions (Genz and Brabon, 2010) acknowledge and explore how current iterations of feminist theory position gender as just one symbol and cipher of subordination. This more reflexive critique has yet to be acknowledged as a recognised element of the gendered entrepreneurial discourse and interestingly, suggests some fracturing between the theoretical and policy-based strands of thinking. Policy initiatives focused upon women of colour and those from ethnic minority groups have been prioritised within developed economies. Whilst these may arise largely from more instrumental objectives regarding economic participation in the context of poor employment prospects, they have, nevertheless, recognised diversity within the gender debate. Cross-country differences in research in relation to gender and business ownership which takes into consideration the intersection of institutions, gender and race has been limited with Minniti (2009: 557) commenting that, 'studies have been sparse with respect to the issue of why racial and ethnic minority women are underrepresented among self-employed females'.

As noted above, theoretical development in this field has been constrained by the tendency for gender to be used as a generic term within the majority of mainstream theorising (Calás *et al.*, 2009). It is acknowledged that hyper-reflexivity in drilling down to individualised micro performances of gender is probably not helpful as an introductory framing to every discussion of women as business owners. Yet, recognition of the problem of universal definitions of gender is required to progress our understanding of how ascribed characteristics intersect to generate differential matrices of disadvantage. A complementary thread of analysis accompanying the notion of intersectionality is that of context.

10.6 CONTEXT

Welter (2011) notes the importance of context in shaping entrepreneurial opportunities and behaviours. Specifically, she draws attention to institutional influences and constraints which limit – or facilitate – entrepreneurship; for example, the porous nature of institutions within previously socialist economies and how these are infused with corruption at local and national levels. In addition, Welter suggests that how gender is articulated within the entrepreneurial debate has to acknowledge context so, within transitional economies, stereotypical assumptions regarding the position of women as domestic labourers critically shape the strategies they employ to claim legitimacy as entrepreneurial actors. The importance and influence of context is exemplified in Chapter 9 of this text (Al-Dajani and Marlow) which explores the empowering potential of entrepreneuring activities for migrant Palestinian women. Thus, within a context of patriarchy, deprivation and social stigma these women use entrepreneuring to address some aspect of their own and their community's embedded disadvantage. However, context is not a construct which only applies to those economies and situations which differ from the presumed norm of Western developed nations; adopting this stance is both discriminatory and blinkered in that it suggests a dominant model to which others should aspire. Consequently, adopting a more critical appraisal of how context is positioned within current theorising around gender and entrepreneurial behaviours offers potential to progress debate whilst acknowledging that competing and contrasting contextual influences require clearer recognition.

10.7 FINANCE

Given the attention which has been afforded to the interface between gender and finance, it might be supposed that there are few novel options remaining under this particular umbrella. After all, we are well versed in the arguments that women are reluctant borrowers, demand lower levels of finance and make limited use of angel and equity finance (Freel *et al.*, 2012) – it should be noted however, that similar observations can be applied to nearly all business owners. Indeed, analysing the use of finance with gender as a dependent variable is not very helpful as issues such as business age, sector and growth interface with gender in a complex fashion (Fairlie and Robb, 2008). That is not to discount the influence of gender but rather, to recognise the complex manner in which it positions women-owned firms in certain sectors and influences growth trajectories and ambitions et cetera has to be acknowledged and factored into relevant debates around finance. These certainly are being acknowledged within current theorising but there are however, some further and possibly novel areas of debate which might fruitfully be progressed.

Thus, there has been much celebration of micro-finance schemes as particularly suitable for self-employed women (Roodman and Morduch, 2009); such low-risk restricted financial provision accords with stereotypical gendered assumptions regarding women's natural preference for small-scale limited funding. This proposition is worthy of critical examination as a self-fulfilling prophesy such that further empirical work exploring the limiting impact of such schemes is essential. As Desmedt (2010) found, micro finance offers a false promise of enterprise; there is a suggestion of unbounded potential within the entrepreneurial discourse but this is constrained by the very limitations of the funding and related scalability. In particular, micro finance is positioned as an almost evangelical force for good in offering women, particularly those in developing nations, entrepreneuring opportunities such that they might address localised poverty. Exploring the implications of this – that globalised structural poverty can be addressed by micro funding of female enterprise and, that women can and should take responsibility for poverty alleviation – offers considerable potential to critically appraise the gendered assumptions which underpin this debate.

Alternatively, greater explorations of the strategies and experiences of those in developed economies who do pursue funding to grow their firms would be fruitful to explore prevalent assumptions surrounding the pursuit and management of such funding. In addition, to what extent the masculine dominated equity industry and angel network adopt or reflect gendered assumptions within lending decisions is certainly worthy of further analysis. Carter *et al.* (2007) have developed a nuanced critique of gender bias within bank lending decisions; a similar investigation of the relatively unknown arena of equity funding would be both informative and novel.

10.8 SOCIAL ENTREPRENEURSHIP

Social entrepreneurship is regarded as a new and emerging field of enquiry and as such has been subject to both empirical and theoretical attention (Osberg and Martin, 2007). However, despite Haugh's (2005) calls for more gender sensitive studies of social entrepreneurial activity, to date there has been very little academic attention paid to gender or women's social entrepreneurship (Teasdale *et al.*, 2008). Some tentative evidence from UK samples suggests that women are more likely to engage in social entrepreneurship as opposed to commercial entrepreneurship (Harding, 2006). This evidence is based on women's greater propensity to volunteer in comparison to their male counterparts (DiMaggio and Louch, 1998), which is predominantly grounded in societal expectations related to caring, femininity, maternal sentiments and feelings (Bowden and Mummery, 2009). However, the more selfless and caring disposition of women is an essentialist and reductionist explanation for greater levels of women's entrepreneurial activity within the social context (Laure Humbert, 2012). For instance, does this position men in the social enterprise context, by default, as being less caring, less concerned with the social objectives of the organisation and therefore, inherently more attracted or driven by the entrepreneurial aspect of social entrepreneurship? No. Paradoxically, these men tend to be portrayed as social heroes. The hero discourse is not new in entrepreneurship literature (Anderson, 2005) but this heroic nature is exaggerated in the context of social entrepreneurs. Dees (2004, as cited in Chell, 2007) talks of 'unsung heroes', 'alchemists . . . [with] magical qualities . . . [who] build things from nothing'. Furthermore, such individuals may be considered as deviant in the academic literature but this relates to social deviance, an unwillingness to accept the status quo and a potential to bend the rules or engage in unethical activity for the sake of a higher cause: in other words, a 'Robin Hood' positioning of male social entrepreneurs. This construction saves the male social entrepreneur from being considered as lacking in comparison to the hegemonic male of commercial entrepreneurship because, rather than being affiliated with the more feminine 'social' qualities or aspects of social entrepreneurship, the essentialist attractions for females, he remains affiliated with Schumpeter's hegemonic male, engaging in creative destruction of societal inequalities whilst fulfilling protector and provider roles.

So, male social entrepreneurs are positioned as hyper-masculine supermen with women social entrepreneurs making a contribution as a result of, and in addition to, the responsibilities of their domestic spheres. Instead of social entrepreneurship offering a more open or accessible space for women's entrepreneurial activity as opposed to the commercial arena, it seems to be a highly gendered space where polar binaries are reflected in the discourses (McAdam and Treanor, 2012). Thus, research whereby gender is used as a lens and not merely as a variable is required to overcome the current 'malestream' social entrepreneurship discourse. Such research should focus on establishing the reality of women's socially entrepreneurial activity, in terms of incidence, sector and scale, whilst also offering insight into the multiplicity of women's backgrounds, experiences and motivations in engaging with this activity. In this way, the nature of women's contribution and impact in this sector can be illuminated and better supported.

10.9 EDUCATION

Entrepreneurship education has emerged in recent years as increasingly important within the matrix of pedagogical provision provided by universities and to a lesser extent, secondary education. As such, the impetus for this rests with the notion of promoting more enterprising attitudes amongst younger people regardless of whatever career they pursue but also, to position business creation as a desirable and feasible option. In effect, the student body are being alerted to the necessity of creating the 'enterprising self' whilst the persona of the entrepreneur is afforded enhanced status and positioned as a desirable and accessible subject being. However, work by Jones (2011) has revealed the gendered bias which pervades current approaches to entrepreneurship education. In essence, this bias is reproduced upon a number of levels – how the entrepreneur is represented and displayed within current teaching programmes, how students absorb and reproduce popularised notions of who is and who can be an entrepreneur and also, the nature of the activities they undertake to 'learn' about entrepreneurship. Such bias neatly fits with the contemporary masculinised discourse of entrepreneurship to recreate a narrow, confirmatory and closed sense of the possibilities within entrepreneurship. Given the vital importance of future enactments of entrepreneuring where the role and status of the entrepreneur is feted throughout society, almost as a modern day hero, excluding potential heroines is problematic. Thus, one of the global concerns regarding entrepreneurship remains women's underrepresentation yet, it would appear that the subtext embedded within the education process is that of bias and exclusion. Consequently, greater critical engagement with how entrepreneurship is portrayed and articulated within the university curriculum is of much interest.

The substantive issues outlined above are only a few examples where potential lies for future exploration; in addition, we might add gendered succession in family firms, women as high technology venturers, relationships between gender and firm growth, the influence of gender upon internationalisation, entrepreneurship as a life course event rather than a life time career et cetera. However, a key element to this debate lies with how knowledge is progressed through empirical investigation and so we explore this in a little more depth.

10.10 RESEARCHING GENDER AND ENTREPRENEURSHIP

As has already been noted above, as the literature regarding gender and entrepreneurship developed there was a notable tendency to position gender as a variable with the focus upon measuring gender differences. The ontological perspective underpinning much of this work uncritically presumed upon entrepreneurship as gender neutral and in addition, reflecting stereotypical assumptions, women's businesses would underperform. As Ahl (2006) noted, this assumption fuelled a self-fulfilling prophecy as researchers presumed upon female deficit, sought it out and exaggerated it if necessary to satisfy social expectations. Whilst gender as an issue was recognised, prevailing ontological and epistemological stances embedded the notion that women could only be included on the research agenda as an adjunct of men and moreover, assumptions of lack critically shaped the empirical enquiry. It is noted however, that whilst gender as a variable can be useful for global overviews of populations and should feature in analyses of large data sets, associated outcomes require reflective critique to avoid limiting and gender biased interpretations. Indeed, recent work such as that of the Global Entrepreneurship Monitor (Hart and Levie, 2011) demonstrates far greater gender reflexivity. Consequently, quantitative analyses of the relationship between gender and entrepreneuring are critical to illustrate change and associated trends over time yet, how these outcomes are represented and interpreted must be sensitive to embedded gender bias. Much scope exists in offering critical evaluations of normative approaches within the positivist tradition to advance current understandings of the 'bigger' picture.

It is noted that much of the existing work on gender and entrepreneuring reflects an interpretative qualitative approach utilising small self-reported samples. This in itself has been useful to offer a fine grained overview of how women engage with entrepreneuring behaviours but there has been some tendency for fairly limited description to ensue (Neergaard et al., 2011). So, as Calás et al. (2009) argue, to progress debate, analyses grounded in feminist theory are essential to develop informed conceptual critiques of the relationship between gender and entrepreneuring. Only by adopting a feminist gaze that considers women as worthy research subjects in and of themselves can there be any challenge to embedded ontological assumptions. Consequently, future research has to move beyond descriptive accounts which assume upon a masculine norm. In addition to developing a more critical utilisation of both quantitative and qualitative data informed by feminist analyses, there would be much scope in focusing upon longitudinal work. This might be through periodic data gathering, building life history narratives or through detailed and ongoing case study construction. There is a dearth of longitudinal studies which explore how women's experience of entrepreneuring changes over time – this is particularly important given current work on the life course. Accordingly, there is much scope to develop far greater critical reflexivity within current approaches to studying the relationship between gender and entrepreneurship.

10.11 CONCLUDING REMARKS

Within this text, we have not adopted a universal view of 'woman' which denies diversity and ignores agency (Earle and Letherby, 2003). Rather, we consider women to be a heterogeneous group and as such acknowledge that ethnicity, culture, class and education will all influence women's experiences of business ownership. However, it would be beyond our scope here to provide an account of global female entrepreneurship and so, we predominately focus on the experiences of UK, European and North American female entrepreneurs. However, we note the limitations of this approach and indeed, draw attention to the need for future research to recognise the Euro–US-centric dominance in current research efforts. Yet, whilst acknowledging the bounded nature of the discussion, it does span a diverse range of related issues which confirm the complexity and scope of exploring the relationship between gender and entrepreneurial activities and ambitions.

It is evident from this text that women, who as a universal group are representative of the notion of gender, have been positioned as a discrete and separate category within the contemporary entrepreneurial discourse. The mere fact that they are labelled as 'female' entrepreneurs or 'women' business owners is testament to this fact; indeed, this confirms that there are normal entrepreneurs (men, family teams, partnerships) and separate from them, are women. As a special and distinct category, much attention has been afforded to strategies whereby women can be fixed and their alleged shortcomings addressed. Whilst contemporary critiques (Ahl, 2006; Ahl and Marlow, 2012; Marlow and McAdam, 2012) demonstrate that such shortcomings are a manufactured reflection of social assumptions and expectations and in fact, there are few gender-based firm performance differences – yet the deficit model persists. Hence, given the normative model of masculinity, this requires women to emulate the behaviours of men but, in order to retain and respect the gender binary – fundamental to social ordering – not *too* much like men. So, women business owners are a conundrum which evokes a paradox. To encourage and exploit their potential to contribute to the contemporary entrepreneurial project, it appears that they must be equipped with the appropriate skills which reflect those inherent within men yet, critical research suggests there are more gendered similarities than differences. Accordingly, there is a status afforded to the normative entrepreneur to which women must aspire but in fact, can never reach as it is largely mythical. However, in drawing our arguments together we are wary of a sense of gender denial; this is not the intention. Rather, gender subordination occurs when women are presumed to be different (weaker); that these weaknesses are axiomatically exhibited within entrepreneurship and so require special fixing. Such assumptions are clear articulations of gendered disadvantage. We also recognise that a gendered socioeconomic context does exclude women from certain sectors of the economy

105

associated with higher status entrepreneuring such as innovative technology, biological medicine, engineering et cetera. Again however, we would argue that limitations within access to education and career development prior to entrepreneuring are the critical gendered influences here – not some type of failure by women to engage with such sectors. Thus, gender is an embedded ascription which shapes women's role and visibility within the socio-economic context; entrepreneurship is but one articulation of disadvantage and must be seen as such.

However, in drawing together these arguments, we would suggest that exploring and analysing gender is critical not only to expose how men and women are positioned within the contemporary entrepreneurial agenda but also, the broader implications of this biased positioning. In effect, entrepreneurship is feted as an open site of egoistic market activity in that it allegedly represents the expression of autonomous agency where opportunity is not bounded by normative institutional constraints (Calás *et al.*, 2009). As such, it is presented as 'de-instiutionalised' (Heintz and Nadai, 1998) as an individualised agentic project. Thus, attainment and achievement in this field is popularly represented as an outcome of individual effort and applied determination (Radu and Redien-Collot, 2008); as such, entrepreneurship is deemed to offer a meritocratic field of socio-economic possibilities within the contemporary postmodern project (McRobbie, 2009). This representation has been revealed as simplistic and mythical; critical analyses of the entrepreneurial discourse suggest that the contemporary image of the successful entrepreneurial character is persistently male (Ogbor, 2000; Ahl, 2006; Taylor and Marlow, 2009). This arises from the gendered affiliation between stereotypical masculinity and entrepreneurial attributes (aggression, competitiveness, risk taking) (Eddleston and Powell, 2008). The mapping of masculinity onto entrepreneuring produces and reproduces a gendered site of activity and identity. Thus, entrepreneurship is defined in contradiction; an open, meritocratic site of economic agency which is however, embedded in masculinity.

This argument has a number of implications; despite an assumption that entrepreneurship heralds a new form of gender neutral opportunity seeking economic behaviour, it reproduces the gender binary. Thus, women are particularly vulnerable within the contemporary entrepreneurial project. Although encouraged to engage with new forms of socio-economic participation which ostensibly reflect individualised postfeminist opportunities, a gendered entrepreneurial regime persists which reproduces subordinated heteronormativity. Consequently, this ostensibly open and agentic site of activity which purports to be accessible to all willing to pursue their individual ambitions is a masquerade which potentially positions women as deficient members of a gendered outgroup. And even for those who demonstrate the most diligent agentic efforts to become business owners, they remain for ever defined as other – the *female* entrepreneur. Finally, this text explores a number of different avenues regarding the role and position of women business owners; their experiences of entrepreneuring has been critically analysed through a gendered lens which illustrates the masculine bias which prevails. Clearly, entrepreneurial activities also represent new fields of opportunity for women – just as they successfully navigate through managerial and professional careers, so they will do so in this field and in so doing, offer a valuable contribution. So, we do not suggest that gender discrimination undermines any contribution that women might make to contemporary entrepreneurial activity but rather, we need to develop an ongoing critique which exposes the conditions under which contribution is made.

Notes

1 SETTING THE SCENE

1   Such owners/shareholders have a dominant control over the business, are involved in day-to-day ctivities of the venture and the business is a going concern.
2   Women's contribution to family business will be discussed in detail in Chapter 5.
3   According to *Global Entrepreneurship Monitor*, this rate in most countries is approximately 30 per cent (Minniti *et al.*, 2005).

2 THE SOCIO-ECONOMIC CONTEXT OF FEMALE ENTREPRENEURSHIP

1   Ireland, France and Japan were much later in legalising the contraceptive pill (Hakim, 1991).
2   This is contrary to the liberal feminism approach which posits that once structural barriers such as sex discrimination are removed women should be able to hold higher status positions.

4 FEMINIST METHODOLOGICAL APPROACHES

1   A complete overview of feminist theory is not the aim of the chapter but rather the provision of a summary of the main schools of thought and their relevance to researching female entrepreneurship.
2   This popular self-help book by John Gray, takes the standpoint that men and women are essentially defined as beings from different planets.

8 NEW SITES OF WOMEN'S ENTREPRENEURSHIP: HIGH TECHNOLOGY ENTREPRENEURSHIP

1   Critical mass: the notion that once there are sufficient numbers of women in SET, traditional masculine norms and traditions will diminish.

9 EMPOWERMENT THROUGH ENTREPRENEURSHIP

1 Born Rania Yaseen, to a displaced Palestinian family living in Kuwait
   (www.queenrania.jo).

References

Achenhagen, L. and Welter, F. (2003) Female entrepreneurship in Germany: context development and its reflection in German media. In J.E. Butler (Ed.), *New Perspective on Women Entrepreneurs*. US: Information Age Publishing.

Acker, J. (1992) Gendering organisational theory. In A. Mills and P. Tancred (Eds), *Gendering Organisational Analysis*. London: Sage.

Acs, Z.J., Arenuis, P., Hay, M. and Minniti, M. (2005) *Global Entrepreneurship Monitor: 2004 executive report*. Available at: http://www.gemconsortium.org

Adib, A. and Guerrier, Y. (2003) The interlocking of gender with nationality, race, ethnicity and class: the narratives of women in hotel work. *Gender Work and Organization*, 10(4): 413–432.

Adkins, L. (2002) *Revisions: Gender and Sexuality in Late Modernity*. Buckingham: Open University Press.

Adler, N.J. and Izraeli, D. (1988) *Women in Management Worldwide*. Armonk, NY: M.E. Sharp.

Adler, N.J. and Izraeli, D. (1994) *Competitive Frontiers: Women Managers in a Global Economy*. Cambridge, MA: Blackwell.

Ahl, H.J. (2004) *The Scientific Reproduction of Gender Inequality: A Discourse Analysis of Research Texts upon Women's Entrepreneurship*. Copenhagen: CBS Press.

Ahl, H.J. (2006) Why research on women entrepreneurs needs new directions. *Entrepreneurship Theory and Practice*, 30(5): 595–621.

Ahl, H.J. (2007) Sex business in the toy store: a narrative analysis of a teaching case. *Journal of Business Venturing*, 22: 673–693.

Ahl, H. and Marlow, S. (2012) Gender and entrepreneurship research: employing feminist theory to escape the dead end. *Organization*, forthcoming.

Ahl, H. and Nelson, T. (2010) Moving forward: institutionalised perspectives on gender and entrepreneurship. *International Journal of Gender and Entrepreneurship*, 2(1): 5–9.

Al-Budirate, A. (2009) *Jordanian Experience in Measuring Employment in the Informal Sector*. Paper presented to the Global Forum on Gender Statistics, United Nations Statistics Organisation, Accra.

Al-Dajani, H. (2007) *Women's Empowerment: A Comparison between Non-profit and For-profit Approaches in Empowering Home-based Women Producers*. Unpublished PhD thesis, University of Strathclyde, Glasgow.

Al-Dajani, H. and Carter, S. (2010) Women empowering women: how female entrepreneurs support home-based producers in Jordan. In C. Brush, A. De Bruin, E. Gatewood and C. Henry (Eds), *Women Entrepreneurs and the Global Environment for Growth: A Research Perspective* (pp. 118–137). Northampton: Edward Elgar.

Al-Dajani, H. and Marlow, S. (2010) The impact of women's home-based enterprise on marriage dynamics: evidence from Jordan. *International Small Business Journal*, 28(5): 470–487.

Aldrich, H. (2000) Learning together: national differences in entrepreneurship research. In D. Sexton and H. Landström (Eds), *The Blackwell Handbook of Entrepreneurship* (pp. 5–25). London: Blackwell.

Aldrich, H. and Cliff, J. (2003) The pervasive effects of family on entrepreneurship toward a family embeddedness perspective. *Journal of Business Venturing*, 18: 573–596.

Aldrich, H. and Fiol, M. (1994) Fools rush in? The institutional context of industry creation. *Academy of Management Review*, 19: 645–670.

Aldrich, H. and Zimmer, C. (1986) Entrepreneurship through social networks. In D.L. Sexton and R.W. Smilor (Eds), *The Art and Science of Entrepreneurship*. Cambridge, MA: Ballinger.

Aldrich, H., Elam, A.B. and Reece, P.R. (1997) Strong ties, weak ties and strangers: do women owners differ from men in their use of networking to obtain assistance?' In S. Birley and I.C. MacMillan (Eds), *Entrepreneurship in a Global Context*. London: Routledge.

Aldrich, J. (1989) Networking among women entrepreneurs. In O. Hagan, C. Rivchum and D. Sexton (Eds), *Women Owned Businesses* (pp. 103–132). New York: Praeger.

Allen, B.J. (2003) *Difference Matters: Communicating Social Identity in Organization*. Prospects Heights, IL: Waveland.

Allen, E., Langowitz, N. and Minniti, M. (2007) *The 2006 Global Entrepreneurship Monitor Special Topic Report: Women in Entrepreneurship*. Babson Park, MA: Center for Women Leadership, Babson College.

Alsos, G.A., Isaksen, E.J. and Ljunggren, E. (2006) New venture funding and subsequent business growth in men- and women-led businesses. *Entrepreneurship, Theory and Practice*, 30(5): 667–683.

Alvesson, M. (1998) Gender relations and identity at work: a case study of masculinities and feminities in an advertising agency. *Human Relations*, 51(8): 113–126.

Alvesson, M. and Due Billing, Y. (1999) *Kon och organisation* [Gender and organisation]. Lund: Studentlitteratur.

Amarapurkar, S.S. and Danes, S.M. (2005) Farm business owning couples: interrelationships among business tensions, relationship conflict quality, and satisfaction with spouse. *Journal of Family and Economic Issues*, 26(3): 419–441.

111

Amatucci, F. and Sohl, J. (2004) Women entrepreneurs securing business angel financing: tales from the field. *Venture Capital: An International Journal of Entrepreneurial Finance*, 6: 181–196.

Anderson, A.R. (2005) Enacted metaphor: the theatricality of the entrepreneurial process. *International Small Business Journal*, 23: 585–603.

Anna, A., Chandler, G., Jansen, E. and Mero, N. (1999) Women business owners in traditional and non-traditional industries. *Journal of Business Venturing*, 15(2): 279–303.

Arenius, P. and Kovalainen, A. (2006) Similarities and differences across the factors associated with women's self employment preference in the Nordic countries. *International Small Business Journal*, 24(1): 31–57.

Arenius, P. and Minniti, M. (2005) Perceptual variables and nascent entrepreneurship. *Small Business Economics*, 24(3): 233–247.

Armstrong, M., Cummins, A., Hastings, S. and Wood, W. (2003) *Job Evaluation: A Guide to Achieving Equal Pay*. London and Sterling, VA: Kogan Page.

Ashcraft, K.L. (2009) Gender and diversity: other ways to make a difference. In M. Alvesson, M. Bridgman and T. Willmott (Eds), *Oxford Handbook of Critical Management Studies* (pp. 304–327). Oxford: Oxford University Press.

Ashcraft, K.L. (2011) Knowing work through the communication of difference: a revised agenda for difference studies. In D.K. Mumby (Ed.), *Reframing Difference in Organizational Communication Studies: Research, Pedagogy, Practice* (pp. 3–29). Thousand Oaks, CA: Sage.

Athayde, R. (2009) Measuring enterprise potential in young people. *Entrepreneurship Theory and Practice*, 33(2): 481–500.

BADIL (2002) *Survey of Palestinian Refugees and Internally Displaced Persons*. BADIL Resource, Centre for Palestinian Residency and Refugee Rights, Bethlehem.

Baines, S., Wheelock, J. (1999) *A Business in the Family: An Investigation of the Contribution of Family to Small Business Survival, Maintenance and Growth*. Institute of Small Business Affairs, Research Series, Monograph No. 3.

Baines, S. and Wheelock, J. (2000) Work and employment in small businesses: perpetuating and challenging gender traditions. *Gender Work and Organisation*, 7(1): 45–56.

Baker, T., Aldrich, H. and Liou, N. (1997) Invisible entrepreneurs: the neglect of women business owners by mass media and scholarly journals in the USA. *Entrepreneurship and Regional Development*, 9(2): 221–238.

Barnes, L.B. (1988) Incongruent hierarchies: daughters and younger sons in company CEOs. *Family Business Review*, 1(1): 9–22.

Barnett, F. and Barnett, S. (1988) *Working Together: Entrepreneurial Couples*. Berkeley, CA: Ten Speed Press.

Barney, J., Busenitz, L., Fiet, J. and Moesel, D. (1996). New venture teams: assessment of learning assistance from venture capital firms. *Journal of Business Venturing*, 11: 257–272.

Bates, T., Jackson, W.E. III and Johnson, J.H. Jr (2007) Introduction to the special issue on advancing research on minority entrepreneurship. *Annals of the American Academy of Political Science and Social Science*, 613: 10–17.

Batliwala, S. (2007) Taking the power out of empowerment – an experiential account. *Development in Practice*, 17(4–5): 557–565.

Battisti, M. and McAdam, M. (2012) The challenges of social capital development within the university science incubator: the case of the graduate entrepreneur. *International Journal of Entrepreneurship and Innovation*, forthcoming.

Baughn, C.C., Chua, B.L. and Neupert, K.E. (2006) The normative context for women's participation in entrepreneruship: a multicountry study. *Entrepreneurship Theory and Practice*, 30: 687–708.

Baxter, J. (1997) Gender equality and participation in housework: a cross-national perspective. *Journal of Comparative Family Studies*, 28: 220–247.

Baxter, J. (2000) The joys and the justice of housework. *Sociology*, 34(4): 609–631.

Baxter, J. and Wright, E.O. (2000) The glass ceiling hypothesis: a comparative study of the United States, Sweden and Australia. *Gender and Society*, 14(2): 275–294.

Beasley, C. (2005) *Gender and Sexuality: Critical Theories, Critical Thinkers*. London: Sage.

Beck, C. (1992) *The Risk Society*. London: Sage.

Becker, G.S. (1964) *Human Capital*. New York: Columbia University Press.

Becker-Blease, J. and Sohl, J. (2007) Do women-owned businesses have equal access to angel capital?' *Journal of Business Venturing*, 22: 503–521.

Belle, A. and La Valle, I. (2003) *Combining Self Employment and Family Life*. Cambridge: Policy Press and Joseph Rowntree Foundation.

Bem, S.L. (1981) *Bem Sex Role Inventory*. Palo Alto, CA: Mind Garden.

Bem, S.L. (1993) *The Lenses of Gender: Transforming the Debate on Sexual Inequality*. New Haven, CT: Yale University Press.

Benschop, Y., Halsema, L. and Schreurs, P. (2001) The division of labour and inequalities between the sexes: an ideological dilemma. *Gender, Work and Organisations*, 8(1): 1–18.

Berg, N. (1997) Gender, place and entrepreneurship. *Entrepreneurship and Regional Development*, 9(3): 259–268.

Berk, S.F. (1985) *The Gender Factor: The Apportionment of Work in American Households*. New York: Plenum.

Berlin, M. (1998) That thing venture capitalists do. *Business Review*, Federal Reserve Bank of Philadelphia, Jan/Feb: 15–26.

Bhide, A. (2000) *The Origin and Evolution of New Businesses*. New York: Oxford University Press.

Bianchi, S.M. and Casper, L.M. (2000) *American Families* (Population Bulletin Vol. 55 No. 4). Washington, DC: Population Reference Bureau.

Bielby, W.T., Baron, J.N. (1984) A woman's place is with other women: sex segregation within organisations. In Barbara Reskin (Ed.), *Sex Segregation in the Workplace:*

Trends, Explorations, Remedies (pp. 27–55). Washington, DC: National Academy Press.

Bird, B. and Brush, C. (2002) A gendered perspective in organisational creation. *Entrepreneurship, Theory and Practice*, 26(3): 41–65.

Birley, S. (1985) The role of networks in the entrepreneurial process. *Journal of Business Venturing*, 1: 107–117.

Björkman, C., Christoff, I., Palm, F. and Vallin, A. (1998) Exploring the pipeline: towards an understanding of the male dominated computing culture and its influence on women. *SIGCSE Bulletin*, 30(2): 64–69.

Bjuggren, P., Melin, L., Ericsson, A., Hall, A., Haag, K., Nordqvist, M. (2004) Ägarskiften och ledarskiften i företag: En fördjupad analys. *NUTEK.B*: Stockholm: Nutek.

Blackburn, R. and Smallbone, D. (2008) Researching small firms and entrepreneurship in the UK: developments and distinctiveness. *Entrepreneurship Theory and Practice*, 32(2): 267–288.

Blackwell, L. and Glover, J. (2008) Women's scientific employment and family formation: a longitudinal perspective. *Gender, Work and Organization*, 15(6): 579–599.

Blanchflower, D.G. and Shadforth, C. (2007) Entrepreneurship in the UK. *Foundations and Trends in Entrepreneurship*, 3(4): 257–364.

Boden, R.J. (1998) Gender and self-employment selection: an empirical assessment. *Journal of Socioeconomics*, 25: 671–682.

Boden, R.J. and Nucci, A. (2000) On the survival prospects of men's and women's new business ventures. *Journal of Business Venturing*, 15(4): 347–362.

Bohan, J.S. (1993) Essentialism, constructionism, and feminist psychology. *Psychology of Women Quarterly*, 17(1): 5–21.

Bolton, S.C. and Muzio, D. (2008) The paradoxical processes of feminization in the professions: the case of established aspiring and semi-professions. *Work, Employment and Society*, 22(2): 281–299.

Bordat, S.W., Schaefer Davis, S. and Kouzzi, S. (2011) Women as agents of grassroots change: illustrating micro-empowerment in Morocco. *Journal of Middle East Women's Studies*, 7(1): 90–119.

Bosma, N. and Harding, R. (2006) *GEM 2006 Summary Results*, Babson College, MA; London Business School. Available at: www.gemconsortium.org

Bosma, N. and Levie, J. (2009) *GEM 2009 Summary Results*. Babson College, MA; London Business School. Available at: www.gemconsortium.org

Bourdieu, P. (1977) *Outline of Theory of Practice*. Cambridge: Cambridge University Press.

Bourdieu, P. (1990) *The Logic of Practice*. Stanford, CA: Stanford University Press.

Bourdieu, P. (2001) *Masculine Domination*. Cambridge: Polity Press.

Bowden, P. and Mummery, J. (2009) *Understanding Feminism*. New York: Acumen.

Bradley, H. (2007) *Gender*. London: Polity Press.

Bradley, H., Erickson, M., Stephenson, C. and Williams, S. (Eds) (2000) *Myths at Work*. Cambridge: Polity Press.

Brindley, C. (2005) Barriers to women achieving their entrepreneurial potential. *International Journal of Entrepreneurial Behaviour and Research*, 11(2): 144–161.

Broadbridge, A. and Simpson, R. (2011) 25 years on: reflecting on the past and looking to the future in gender and management research. *British Journal of Management*, 22: 470–483.

Bruce, D. (1999) Do husbands matter? Married women entering self-employment. *Small Business Economics*, 13(4): 317–329.

Bruni, A., Gherardi, S. and Poggio, B. (2004a) Entrepreneur-mentality, gender and the study of women entrepreneurs. *Journal of Organisational Change Management*, 17(3): 256–268.

Bruni, A., Gherardi, S. and Poggio, B. (2004b) Doing gender, doing entrepreneurship: an ethnographic account of intertwined practices. *Gender, Work and Organisation*, 11: 406–429.

Bruni, A., Gherardi, S. and Poggio, B. (2005) *Gender and Entrepreneurship: An Ethnographic Approach*. London: Routledge.

Brush, C. (1992) Research on women business owners: past trends, a new perspective and future directions. *Entrepreneurship, Theory and Practice*, 16(4): 5–30.

Brush, C. and Chaganti, R. (1998) Business with glamour? An analysis of resources of performance by size and age in small service and retail firms. *Journal of Business Venturing*, 14: 233–257.

Brush, C., Greene, P.G. and Hart, M. (2001a) From initial idea to unique advantage: the entrepreneurial challenge of constructing a resource base. *Academy of Management Executive*, 15(1): 64–80.

Brush, C., Carter, N., Gatewood, E., Green, P. and Hart, M. (2001b) 'The Diana Project': *Women Business Owners and Equity Capital: The Myths Dispelled*. Insight Report. Kansas City, MO: Kauffman Center for Entrepreneurial Leadership.

Brush, C., Carter, N., Greene, P.G., Hart, M. and Gatewood, E.J. (2002) The role of social capital and gender in linking financial suppliers and entrepreneurial firms: a framework for future research. *Venture Capital*, 4(4): 305–323.

Brush, C., Carter, N., Gatewood, E., Green, P.G. and Hart, M. (2004) *Clearing the Hurdles: Women Building High Growth Businesses*. Upper Saddle River, NJ: FT/Prentice Hall.

Brush, C., Carter, N., Gatewood, E., Green, P. and Hart, M. (2006) The use of boot-strapping by women entrepreneurs in positioning got growth. *Venture Capital: An International Journal*, 8(1): 15–31.

Brush, C., De Bruin, A. and Welter, F. (2009) A gender-aware framework for women's entrepreneurship. *International Journal of Gender and Entrepreneurship*, 1(1): 8–24.

Buitelaar, M. (2007) Staying close by moving out: the contextual meanings of personal autonomy in the life stories of women of Moroccan descent in the Netherlands. *Contemporary Islam*, 1: 3–22.

Buller, R.E. (2007) Un/Veiled: feminist art from the Arab/Muslim diaspora. *Al-Raida*, 24(116–117): 16–20.

Burt, R. (2000) The network structure of social capital. In R.I. Sutton and B.M. Straw (Eds), *Research in Organizational Behaviour* (pp. 45–423). Greenwich, CT: JAI Press.

Busentiz, L.W., Fiet, J.O. and Moesel, D.D. (2004) Reconsidering the venture capitalists' 'value added' proposition: an interorganizational learning perspective. *Journal of Business Venturing,* 19: 787–807.

Butler, J. (1990) *Gender Trouble.* London: Routledge.

Butler, J. (1993) *Bodies that Matter: On the Discursive Limits of Sex.* New York: Routledge.

Butler, J. (1997) *Excitable Speech — a Politics of the Performative.* London: Routledge.

Butler, J. (2004) *Undoing Gender.* New York: Routledge.

Buttner, E.H. (1993) Female entrepreneurs: how far have they come? *Business Horizons,* 36(2): 59–65.

Buttner, E.H. and Rosen, B. (1992) Perception in the loan application process: male and female entrepreneurs, perceptions and subsequent intentions. *Journal of Small Business Management,* January: 58–65.

Bygrave, W.D., Hay, M., Ng, E. and Reynolds, P. (2002) *A study of informal investing in 29 nations comprising the Global Entrepreneurship Monitor.* Frontiers in Entrepreneurship Research.

Byrnes, J.P., Miller, D.C. and Schafer, W.D. (1999) Gender differences in risk taking: a meta-analysis. *Psychological Bulletin,* 125(3): 367–383.

Cachon, J.C. (1990) *A Longitudinal Investigation of Entrepreneurial Teams.* Paper presented at Babson Entrepreneurship Research Conference, Babson.

Calás, M. and Smircich, L. (1996) From the woman's point of view: feminist approaches to organisation studies. In S. Clegg, C. Hardy and W. Nord (Eds), *Handbook of Organisation Studies* (pp. 218–257). London: Sage.

Calás, M.B., Smircich, L. and Bourne, K.A. (2009) Extending the boundaries: reframing 'entrepreneurship as social change' through feminist perspectives. *Academy of Management Review,* (34)3: 552–569.

Cantillon, R. (1755) *Essay on the Nature of Commerce.* H. Higgs translation, 1931. London: Macmillan.

Caputo, R.K. and Dolinksky, A. (1998) Women's choice to pursue self-employment: the role of financial and human capital of household members. *Journal of Small Business Management,* 36(3): 8–17.

Carli, L.L. and Eagly, A.H. (2001) Gender, hierarchy, and leadership: an introduction. *Journal of Social Issues,* 57(4): 629–636.

Carr, D. (1996) Two paths to self-employment? Women's and men's self-employment in the United States, 1980. *Work and Occupations,* 23: 26–53.

Carter, N.M. and Allen, K.R. (1997) Size determinants of women-owned business: choices or barriers to resources. *Entrepreneurial and Regional Development,* 9(3): 211–220.

Carter, N.M., Brush, C.G., Green, P.G. and Hart, M.M. (2003) Women entrepreneurs who break through the equity financing: the influence of human, social and financial capital. *Venture Capital,* 5(1): 237–251.

Carter, S. (1993) Female business ownership: current research and possibilities for the future. In S. Allen and C. Truman (Eds), *Women in Business: Perspectives on Women Entrepreneurs* (pp. 148–160). London: Routledge.

Carter, S. (2000) Gender and enterprise. In S. Carter and D. Jones-Evans (Eds), *Enterprise and Small Business: Principles, Practice and Policy.* London: Prentice Hall.

Carter, S. and Rosa, P. (1998) The financing of male and female owned businesses. *Entrepreneurship and Regional Development,* 10: 225–241.

Carter, S. and Shaw, E. (2006) *Women's Business Ownership: Recent Research and Policy Development,* London: Small Business Service Research Report. Available at: http://www.berr.gov.uk/files/file38330.pdf

Carter, S., Anderson, S. and Shaw, S. (2001) *Women Business Ownership: A Review of the Academic Popular and Internet Literature.* London: Small Business Service Research Report RR002/01.

Carter, S., Shaw, E., Lam, W. and Wilson, F. (2007) Gender, entrepreneurship, and bank lending: the criteria and processes used by bank loan officers in assessing applications. *Entrepreneurship Theory and Practice,* 31(3): 427–444.

Cassar, G. (2001) The financing and capital structure of business start-ups: the importance of asset structure. In W. Bygrave, E. Autio, C. Brush, P. Davidsson, P. Greene, P. Reynolds and H. Sapienza (Eds), *Frontiers of Entrepreneurship Research.* Wellesley, MA: Babson College.

Catalyst (2006) *2006 Catalyst Census of Women Board Directors of the Fortune 1000.* Available at: http://catalystwomne.org/index.htm

CAWTAR (2007) *Women Entrepreneurs in: MENA: Characteristics, Contributions and Challenges.* Tunis: Centre for Arab Women's Training and Research.

Cejka, M.A. and Eagly, A.H. (1999) Gender stereotypic image of occupations correspond to the sex segregation of employment. *Personality and Social Psychology Bulletin,* 25: 413–423.

Cerulo, K. (1997) Identity construction: new issues, new directions. *Annual Review of Sociology,* 23: 385–409.

Chant, S. (2008) The 'feminisation of poverty' and the 'feminisation' of anti-poverty programmes: room for revision? *Journal of Development Studies,* 44(2): 165–197.

Chant, S. and Pedwell, C. (2008) *Women, Gender and the Informal Economy: An Assessment of ILO Research and Suggested Ways Forward.* International Labour Organisation (ILO) Discussion Paper. Geneva: ILO.

Charles, M. (2003) Deciphering sex segregation: vertical and horizontal inequalities in ten national labour markets. *Acta Sociologica,* 46: 267–287.

Charles, M. and Grusky, D.B. (2004) *Occupational Ghettos: The Worldwide Segregation of Women and Men.* Stanford, CA: Stanford University Press.

Charrad, M. (2011) Gender in the Middle East: Islam, state, agency. *Annual Review of Sociology*, 37: 417–437.

Chell, E. (2007) Social enterprise and entrepreneurship. *International Small Business Journal*, 25(1): 5–26.

Chell, E. and Baines, S. (1998) Does gender affect business 'performance'? A study of microbusinesses in business services in the UK. *Entrepreneurship and Regional Development*, 10(2): 117–135.

Cheryan, S., Plaut, V.C., Davies, P.G. and Steele, C.M. (2009) Ambient belonging: how stereotypical cues impact gender participation in computer science. *Journal of Personality and Social Psychology*, 97: 1045–1060.

Chifos, C. (2007) The sustainable communities experiment in the United States: insights from three federal-level initiatives. *Journal of Planning Education and Research*, 26(4): 435–449.

Chrisman, J.J., Chua, J.H. and Steier, L.P. (2002) The influence of national culture and family involvement on entrepreneurial perceptions and performance at the state level. *Entrepreneurship, Theory and Practice*, 26(4): 113–130.

CIA (2009) *World Fact Book*. Available at: https://www.cia.gov/library/publications/the-world-factbook/geos/jo.html#People

Cliff, J. (1998) Does one size fit all? Exploring attitudes towards growth, gender and business size. *Journal of Business Venturing*, 13: 523–542.

Cole, P.M. (1997) Women in family business. *Family Business Review*, 10(4): 353–371.

Coleman, S. (2000) Access to capital and terms of credit: a comparison of men and women owned small businesses. *Journal of Small Business Management*, 38(3): 37–52.

Coleman, S. (2007) The role of human and financial capital in the profitability and growth of women owned firms. *Journal of Small Management*, 45(3): 303–319.

Coltrane, S. (2000) Research on household labour: modelling and measuring the social embeddedness of routine family work. *Journal of Marriage Family*, 62(4): 1208–1233.

Cooper, A.C., Gimeno-Gascon, F.J. and Woo, C.Y. (1994) Initial human and financial capital as predictors of new venture performance. *Journal of Business Venturing*, 9(5): 371–395.

Cornwall, A. (2007) Pathways of women's empowerment. *Open Democracy*, available at: http://www.opendemocracy.net/article/pathways_of_womens_empowerment

Cornwall, A. and Anyidoho, N.A. (2010) Introduction: women's empowerment: contentions and contestations. *Development*, 53(2): 144–149.

Cowling, M. and Taylor, M. (2001) Entrepreneurial women and men: two different species? *Small Business Economics*, 16: 167–175.

Crenshaw, K. (1997) Intersectionality and identity politics: learning from violence against women of colour. In M. Lyndon Shanaey and U. Narayan (Eds), *Reconstructing Political Identity* (pp. 178–193). University Park: The Pennsylvania State University Press.

Cromie, S. and Birley, S. (1992) Networking by female business owners in Northern Ireland. *Journal of Business Venturing*, 7(3): 237–251.

Cromie, S. and Hayes, J. (1988) Toward a typology of female entrepreneurs. *The Sociological Review*, 36(1): 87–113.

Cross, S. and Bagilhole, B. (2002) Girls' jobs for the boys? Men, masculinity and non-traditional occupations. *Gender Work and Organisation*, 9(2): 204–226.

Crotty, M. (2001) *The Foundations of Social Research: Meaning and Perspective in the Research Process*. London: Sage.

Crump, B.J. (2004) The culture of computing: does context matter? In F. Sudweeks and C. Ess (Eds), *Cultural Attitudes Towards Technology and Communication*. Proceedings of the Fourth International Conference on Cultural Attitudes Towards Communication and Technology, Karlstad, Sweden, 27 June–1 July (pp. 87–91). Australia: Murdoch University.

Crump, B.J., Logan, K. and McIlroy, A. (2007). Does gender still matter? A study of the views of women in the ICT industry in New Zealand. *Gender, Work and Organization*, 14(4): 349–370.

Curimbaba, F. (2002) The dynamics of women's roles as family business managers. *Family Business Review*, 15(3): 239–252.

Curran, J. and Blackburn, R. (2000) *Researching the Small Enterprise*. London: Sage.

Danes, S.M. and Olson, P.D. (2003) Women's role involvement in family businesses, business tensions, and business success. *Family Business Review*, 16(1): 53–64.

Danhauser, C. (1989) Who's is in the Home Office? *American Demographics*, 21: 50–56.

Davidsson, P. (2003) The domain of entrepreneurship research: some suggestions. In J. Katz and D. Shepherd (Eds), *Cognitive Approaches to Entrepreneurship Research: Advances in Entrepreneurship, Firm Emergence and Growth*, Vol. 6, pp. 315–372. Oxford: Elsevier/JAI Press.

Davidsson, P. and Honig, B. (2003) The role of social and human capital among nascent entrepreneurs. *Journal of Business Venturing*, 18: 310–331.

Deaux, K. and LaFrance, M. (1998) Gender. In D.T. Gilbert, S.T. Fiske and G. Lindzey (Eds), *The Handbook of Social Psychology*, Vol. 1 (pp. 788–827). Boston, MA: McGraw-Hill.

De Beauvoir, S. (1988/1949) *The Second Sex*. London: Pan.

de Bruin, A. and Flint-Hartle, S. (2005) Entrepreneurial women and private capital: the New Zealand perspective. *International Journal of Entrepreneurial Behaviour and Research*, 11(2): 108–128.

de Bruin, A. and Lewis, K. (2004) Toward enriching united career theory: familial entrepreneurship and copreneurship. *Career Development Journal*, 9(7): 638–646.

de Bruin, A., Brush, C. and Welter, F. (2006) Introduction to the Special Issue: Towards Building Cumulative Knowledge on Women's Entrepreneurship. *Entrepreneurship, Theory and Practice*, 30(5): 585–593.

119

de Bruin, A., Brush, C. and Welter, F. (2007) Advancing a framework for coherent research on women's entrepreneurship. *Entrepreneurship, Theory and Practice,* 30(5): 585–594.

De Clercq, D. and Voronov, M. (2009a) Toward a practice perspective of entrepreneurship: entrepreneurial legitimacy as habitus. *International Small Business Journal,* 27: 395–419.

De Clercq, D. and Voronov M. (2009b) The role of domination in newcomer's legitimation as entrepreneurs. *Organisation,* 16(6): 799–827.

De Clercq, D. and Voronov, M. (2009c) The role of cultural and symbolic capital in entrepreneurs: ability to meet expectations about conformity and innovation. *Journal of Small Business Management,* 47(3): 398–420.

De Clercq, D. and Voronov, M. (2011) Sustainability in entrepreneurship: a tale of two logics. *International Small Business Journal,* 29(4): 322–344.

Dees, G. (2004) *Rhetoric, Reality and Research: Building Strong Intellectual Foundations for the Emerging Field of Social Entrepreneurship.* Paper presented at the 2004 Skoll World Forum on Social Entrepreneurship, March 2004, Oxford.

Desmedt, E. (2010) *Trapped in Ideology: The Limitations of Micro-finance in Helping Women Create Viable Enterprises.* Unpublished PhD thesis, University of York, UK.

Dex, S. (2003) *Families and Work in the Twenty-first Century.* York: The Joseph Rowntree Foundation.

DiMaggio, P. and Louch, H. (1998) Socially embedded consumer transactions. *American Sociological Review,* 63: 619–637.

Donnellon, A. and Langowitz, N. (2009) Leveraging women's networks for strategic value. *Strategy and Leadership,* 37(3): 29–36.

Doyle, J. and Paludi, M. (1998) *Sex and Gender: The Human Experience.* San Francisco: McGraw-Hill.

Drakopoulou-Dodd, S. and, Anderson, A.R. (2007) Mumpsimus and the mything of the individualistic entrepreneur. *International Small Business Journal,* 25(4): 341–360.

DTI/Small Business Service (2006) *Annual Small Business Survey.* London: DTI Small Business Service.

Duberley, J. and Carrigan, M. (2012) The career identities of 'mumpreneurs': women's experiences of combining enterprise and motherhood. *International Small Business Journal,* 30. DOI: 10.1177/0266242611435182

Dubini, P. and Aldrich, H. (1991) Personal and extended networks are central to the entrepreneurial process. *Journal of Business Venturing,* 6: 305–313.

du Gay, P.A. (2002) Common power to keep them all in awe: a comment on governance. *Cultural Values,* 6(1&2): 11–27.

Dumas, C.A. (1989) Understanding of father–daughter and father–son dyads in family owned businesses. *Family Business Review,* 2(1): 31–46.

Dumas, C.A. (1992) Integrating the daughter into family business management. *Entrepreneurship, Theory and Practice,* 16(4): 41–56.

Dupuis, A. and de Bruin, A. (2004) Women's business ownership and entrepreneurship. In P. Spoonley, A. Dupuis and A. de Bruin (Eds), *Work and Working in 21st Century New Zealand* (pp. 154–179). Palmerston North: Dunmore Press.

DuRietz, A. and Henrekson, M. (2000) Testing the female underperformance hypotheses. *Small Business Economics,* 14(1): 1–10.

Eagly, A.H., Wood, W. and Diekman, P. (2000) Social role theory of sex differences and similarities: a current appraisal. In T. Eckes and H.M. Trautner (Eds), *The Development Social Psychology of Gender* (pp. 123–174). Mahwah, N.J: Erlbaum.

Earle, S. and Letherby, G. (2003) *Gender, Identity and Reproduction: Social Perspectives.* London: Palgrave.

East, J. (2000) Empowerment through welfare-rights organizing: a feminist perspective. *Affilia,* 15: 311–328.

ECDGEI (2008) *Evaluation on Policy: Promotion of Women Innovators and Entrepreneurship.* DG Enterprise and Industry, European Commission. Available at: http://www.ec.europa.eu/enterprise/dgs/eval.htm

Eddleston, K.A. and Powell, G.N. (2008) The role of gender identity in explaining sex differences in business owner's career satisfier preferences. *Journal of Business Venturing,* 23: 244–256.

Elbert, T.L. (1988) The romance of patriarchy: ideology, subjectivity and postmodern feminist cultural theory. *Cultural Critique,* 10: 19–57.

Epstein, C.F. (1999) Similarity and difference: the sociology of gender distinctions. In J. Saltzman Chafetz (Ed.), *Handbook of the Sociology of Gender* (pp. 45–61). New York: Plenum.

Equalities and Human Rights Commission (2011) Sex and Power: 5,400 women missing from top jobs. Available at: http://www.equalityhumanrights.com/key-projects/sexandpower/

Essers, C. and Benschop, Y. (2007) Enterprising identities: female entrepreneurs of Moroccan and Turkish origin in the Netherlands. *Organisation Studies,* 28(1): 49–69.

Essers, C. and Benschop, Y. (2009) Muslim businesswomen doing boundary work: the negotiation of Islam, gender and ethnicity within entrepreneurial context. *Human Relations,* 62(3): 403–423.

Etzkowitz, H., Kemelgor, C. and Uzzi, B. (2000) *Athena Unbound: The Advancement of Women in Science and Technology.* Cambridge: Cambridge University Press.

Eyben, R. and Napier-Moore, R. (2009) Choosing words with care? Shifting meanings of women's empowerment in international development. *Third World Quarterly,* 30(2): 285–300.

Fairlie, R.W. and Robb, A.M. (2008) Gender differences in business performance: evidence from the characteristics of Business Owners Survey. Available at SSRN: http//ssrn.com/abstract=1260987

Fanek, F. (2005) How Jordan earned foreign aid. *Jordan Times,* 25 October: 9.

Faulkner, W. (2001) The technology question in feminism: a view from feminist technology studies. *Women's Studies International Forum,* 24(1): 79–95.

Faulkner, W., Sorenson, K., Gansmo, H. and Rommes, E. (2004) Gender Inclusion with the ICT Workforce. Available at: http//www.sigis-sit.org (accessed June 2011).

Fay, M. and Williams, L. (1993) Sex of applicant and the availability of business start-up finance. *Australian Journal of Management,* 16(1): 65–72.

Feldman, M.P. (2001) The entrepreneurial event revisited: a firm formation in a regional context. *Industrial and Corporate Change,* 10: 861–891.

Fenstermaker, S. and West, C. (2002) 'Doing difference' revisited: problems, prospects, and the dialogue in feminist theory. In S. Fenstermaker and C. West (Eds), *Doing Gender, Doing Difference.* New York: Routledge.

Ferguson, A. (1989) *Blood at the Root.* London: Pandora.

Ferguson, K.E. (1999) Patriarchy. In H. Tierney (Ed.), *Women's Encyclopaedia,* Vol 2. Westwood, CT: Greenwood.

Fielden, S.L., Davidson, M.J., Dawe, A.J. and Makin, P.J. (2003) Factors inhibiting the economic growth of female owned small businesses in North West England. *Journal of Small Business and Enterprise Development,* 10(2): 152–166.

Fine, C. (2010) *Delusions of Gender.* London: Icon Books.

Firkin, P. (2003) Entrepreneurial capital. In A. de Bruin and A. Dupuis (Eds), *Entrepreneurship: New Perspectives in a Global Age* (pp. 57–75). Aldershot: Ashgate.

Firkin, P., Dupuis, A. and De Bruin, A. (2003) Familial entrepreneurship. In A. de Bruin and A. Dupuis (Eds), *Entrepreneurship: New Perspectives in a Global Age* (pp. 92–108). Ashgate: Aldershot.

Fischer, E.M., Reuber, A.R. and Dyke, L.S. (1993) A theoretical overview and extension of research on sex, gender and entrepreneurship. *Journal of Business Venturing,* 8: 152–168.

Fiske, S.T. (1989) Examining the role of intent: toward understanding its role in stereotyping and prejudice. In J.S. Uleman and J.A. Bargh (Eds), *Unintended Thought* (pp. 253–286). New York: Guilford.

Fitzgerald, M.A. and Muske, G. (2002) Coprenuers: an exploration and comparison to other family businesses. *Family Business Review,* 15(1): 1–16.

Flax, J. (1990) *Thinking Fragments: Psychoanalysis, Feminism and Postmodernism in the Contemporary West.* Berkeley: University of California Press.

Foss, L. (2010) Research on entrepreneur networks: the case for a constructionist feminist theory perspective. *International Journal of Gender and Entrepreneurship,* 2(1): 83–102.

Franke, N., Gruber, M., Harhoff, D. and Henkel, J. (2006) What you are is what you like – similarity biases in venture capitalists' evaluation of start-up teams. *Journal of Business Venturing,* 21(6): 802–826.

Fraser, S. (2005) *Finance for Small and Medium Enterprises: A Report in the 2004 UK Survey of SME Finances.* Coventry: Warwick Business School, University of Warwick.

Freear, J. and Wetzel, W. (1992) The investment attitudes, behaviour, and characteristics of high net worth individuals. In N.C. Churchill, S. Birley, W.D. Bygrave,

D.F. Muzyka, C. Wahlbin and W.E. Wetzel Jr. (Eds), *Frontiers of Entrepreneurship Research* (pp. 374–387). Wellesley, MA: Babson College.

Freel, M., Carter, S., Tagg, S. and Mason, C. (2012) The latent demand for bank debt: characterising discouraged borrowers. *Small Business Economics*, 38(4): 399–418.

Galloway, L., (2011) The experiences of male gay business owners in the UK. *International Small Business Journal*. DOI: 0266242610391324

Galloway, L., Brown, W. and Arenuis, P. (2002) Gender-based differences in entrepreneurial behaviour: a comparative examination of Scotland and Finland. *International Journal of Entrepreneurship and Innovation*, 3(2): 109–119.

Gamba, M. and Kleiner, B. (2001) The old boy's network today. *International Journal of Sociology and Social Policy*, 21(8–9): 101–107.

Gartner, W. (2010) A new path to the waterfall: a narrative on the use of entrepreneurial narrative. *International Small Business Journal*, 28(1): 6–20.

Gatewood, E.G., Carter, N.M., Brush, C.G., Greene, P.G. and Hart, M.M. (2003) *Women Entrepreneurs, their Ventures, and the Venture Capital Industry: An Annotated Bibliography*. Stockholm: ESBRI.

Gatewood, E.J., Brush, C.G., Carter, N.M., Greene, P.G. and Hart, M.M. (2009) Diana: a symbol of women entrepreneur's hunt for knowledge, money and the rewards of entrepreneurship. *Small Business Economics*, 32(2): 129–144.

GEM (2009) *2007 Report on Women and Entrepreneurship*. Babson Park, MA: Global Entrepreneurship Monitor.

Genz, S. and Brabon, B. (2010) *Postfeminism: Cultural Texts and Theories*. Edinburgh: Edinburgh University Press.

Gerson, K. (2002) Moral dilemmas, moral strategies and the transformation of gender: lessons from two generations of work and family change. *Gender and Society*, 16: 8–28.

Gherardi, S. (1995) *Gender, Symbolism and Organizational Cultures*. London: Sage.

Gibb, A.A. (1993) Key factors in the design of policy support for the small and medium enterprise (SME) development process: an overview. *Entrepreneurship and Regional Development*, 5: 1–24.

Gibb, A.A. (2000) Small and medium enterprise development: borrowing from elsewhere? *Journal of Small Business and Enterprise Development*, 7(3): 199–211.

Giddens, A. (1984) *The Constitution of Society: Outline of the Theory of Structuration*. Berkeley: University of California Press.

Giddens, A. (1992) *The Transformation of Intimacy*. Cambridge: Polity Press.

Gill, R. (2011) *Globalization and Intersectionality in US Discourses and Practices of Entrepreneurship*. Paper to the EGOS Symposium, June, Gothenburg, Sweden.

Gill, R. and Ganesh, S. (2007) Empowerment, constraint, and the entrepreneurial self: a study of white women entrepreneurs. *Journal of Applied Communication Research*, 35: 268–293.

Gilligan, C. (1982) *In a Different Voice*. Cambridge, MA: Harvard University Press.

Gillis-Donovan, J. and Moynihan-Brandt, C. (1990) The power of the invisible women in the family business. *Family Business Review*, 3(2): 153–167.

Godwin, L.N., Stevens, C.E. and Brenner, N.B. (2006) Forced to play by the rules? Theorizing how mixed-sex founding teams benefit women entrepreneurs in male-dominated contexts. *Entrepreneurship, Theory and Practice*, 25: 27–39.

Goffee, R. and Scase, R. (1985) *Women in Charge: The Experience of Women Entrepreneurs*. London: Allen & Unwin.

Goffman, E. (1987) *Gender Advertisements*. New York: Harper & Row.

Goulding, K. (2011) Tunisia: feminist fall?' *Open Democracy*. Available at: http://www.opendemocracy.net/5050/kristine-goulding/tunisia-feminist-fall

Granovetter, M. (1973) The strength of weak ties. *American Journal of Sociology*, 78: 1360–1380.

Granovetter, M. (1985) Economic action and social structure: the problem of embeddedness. *American Journal of Sociology*, 91: 481–510.

Greene, F. (2010) Patriarchal ideology of motherhood. In S. O'Reilly (Ed.), *Encyclopaedia of Motherhood*, Vol. 1. London: Sage.

Greene, F., Han, L. and Marlow, S. (2011) Like mother, like daughter? Analyzing maternal influences upon women's entrepreneurial propensity. *Entrepreneurship, Theory and Practice*, DOI: 10.1111/j.1540-6520.2011.00484.x

Greene, P., Brush, C. and Brown, T. (1997) Resource configurations in new ventures: relationships to owner and company characteristics. *Journal of Small Business Strategy*, 8: 25–40.

Greene, P., Brush, C., Hart, M. and Sapariot, P. (1999) *Exploration of the Venture Capital Industry: Is Gender an Issue?* Frontiers of Entrepreneurship Research. Wellesley, MA: Babson College. Available at: www.babson.edu/entrep/fer

Greene, P.G., Brush, C.G., Hart, M.M. and Saparito, P. (2001) Patterns of venture capital funding: is gender a factor? *Venture Capital*, 3(1): 63–83.

Greene, P.G., Hart, M.M., Gatewood, E.J., Brush, C.G. and Carter, N.M. (2003) Women entrepreneurs: moving front and centre – an overview of research and theory. White Paper Series. Boca Raton, FL: US Association for Small Business and Entrepreneurship. Available at: www.usasbe.org/knowledge/whitepapers/greene2003.pdf

Greenfield, S. (2002) *Set Fair: A Report on Women in Science, Engineering and Technology*, London: DTI, UK Government.

Greer, M. and Greene, P. (2003) Feminist theory and the study of entrepreneurship. In J. Butler (Ed.), *New Perspectives on Women Entrepreneurs*. Greenwich, CT: IAP.

Grusky, D.B. and Charles, M. (2001) Is there a worldwide sex segregation regime? In D.B. Grusky (Ed.), *Social Stratification: Class, Race and Gender in Sociological Perspective* (pp. 689–703). Newbury Park, CA: Westview Press.

Guiso, L. and Rustichini, A. (2011) *What Drives Women out of Entrepreneurship? The Joint Role of Testesterone and Culture*. CEPR Discussion Paper 8204. Available at: www.cepr.org/pubs/dps/DP8204.asp

Gupta, V.K., Turban, D.B. and Bhawe, N.M. (2008) The effect of gender stereotype activation on entrepreneurial intentions. *Journal of Applied Psychology*, (93)5: 1053–1061.

Gupta, V.K., Turban, D.B., Wasti, S.A. and Sikdar, A. (2009) The role of gender types in perceptions of entrepreneurs and intentions to become an entrepreneur. *Entrepreneurship, Theory and Practice*, 33(2): 397–417.

Hakim, C. (1991) Grateful slaves and self-made women: fact and fantasy in women's work orientations. *European Sociological Review*, 7: 101–121.

Hakim, C. (1996a) *Key Issues in Women's Work – Female Heterogeneity and the Polarisation of Women's Employment*. London: Athlone.

Hakim, C. (1996b) Labour mobility and employment stability: rhetoric and reality on the sex differential in labour market behaviour. *European Sociological Review*, 12: 1–31.

Hakim, C. (2000) *Work–Lifestyle Choices in the 21st Century: Preference Theory*. Oxford: Oxford University Press.

Hakim, C. (2002) Lifestyle preferences as determinants of women's differentiated labour market careers. *Work and Occupations*, 29(4): 428–459.

Hakim, C. (2003) A new approach to explaining fertility patterns: preference theory. *Population and Development Review*, 29(3): 349–374.

Hakim, C. (2006) Women, careers, and work–life preferences. *British Journal of Guidance and Counselling*, 34(3): 279–294.

Halford, S. and Leonard, P. (2005) Place, space and time: contextualising workplace subjectivities. *Organisation Studies*, 27(5): 657–676.

Hamilton, E. (2006) Whose story is it anyway? Narrative accounts of the role of women in founding and establishing family businesses. *International Small Business Journal*, 24: 253–269.

Hamilton, E. and Smith, R. (2003) The entrepreneuse: a silent entrepreneurial narrative. In *Proceedings of the Small Business and Entrepreneurship Development Conference*, University of Surrey, April 2003 (pp. 183–192). Shipley: European Research Press.

Hampton, A., Cooper, S. and McGowan, P. (2009) Female entrepreneurial networks and networking activity in technology-based ventures: an exploratory study. *International Small Business Journal*, 27(2): 193–214.

Hanson, S. (2003) Geographical and feminist perspectives faced by entrepreneurs. *Geographische Zeitschrift*, 91: 1–23.

Harding, R. (2006) *GEM UK: Social Entrepreneurs Specialist Summary*. London: London Business School.

Harding, S. (1986) *Feminism and Methodology*. Bloomington: Indiana University Press.

Harding, S. (1987) Introduction: is there a feminist method? In S. Harding (Ed.), *Feminism and Methodology*. Milton Keynes: Open University Press.

Harrison, R.T. and Mason, C.M. (2000) Venture capital market complementarities: the links between business angels and venture capital funds in the United Kingdom. *Venture Capital*, 2(3): 223–242.

Harrison, R.T. and Mason, C.M. (2007) Does gender matter? Women business angels and the supply of entrepreneurial finance. *Entrepreneurship, Theory and Practice*, 445–472.

Hart, M. and Levie, J. (2011) *Global Entrepreneurship Monitor (GEM) UK Report.* Aston Business School and Hunter Centre for Entrepreneurship, Strathclyde Business School.

Hartmann, H.I. (1981) The unhappy marriage of Marxism and feminism: towards a more progressive union. In L. Sargent (Ed.), *Women and Revolution: A Discussion of the Unhappy Marriage of Marxism and feminism* (pp. 1–41). Boston: South End Press.

Haugh, H. (2005) A research agenda for social entrepreneurship. *Social Enterprise Journal*, 1(1): 1–12.

Hausmann, R., Tyson, L.D. and Zahidi, S. (2006) *The Global Gender Gap Report 2006.* Cologny/Geneva: World Economic Forum.

Haynes, K. (2010) Other lives in accounting: critical reflections on oral history methodology in action. *Critical Perspectives on Accounting*, 21: 221–231.

Heilman, M.E. (1983) Sex bias in work settings: the lack of fit model. *Research in Organisational Behaviour*, 5: 269–298.

Heilman, M.E. (2001). Description and prescription: how gender stereotypes prevent women's ascent up the organizational ladder. *Journal of Social Issues*, 57: 657–674.

Heliman, M.E. and Chen, J.J. (2003) Entrepreneurship as a solution: The allure of self-employment for women and minorities. *Human Resource Management Review*, 13: 347–365.

Heilman, M.E. and Wallen, A.S. (2004) Penalties for success: reactions to women who succeed at male gender typed tasks. *Journal of Applied Psychology*, 89(3): 416–427.

Heintz, B. and Nadai, E. (1998) Geschlect und Kontext – De- institutionalisierungsporzese und Geschlectliche Differenzierung. *Zeitschrift fur Soziologie*, 27(2): 75–93.

Helibrunn, M. (2004) Impact of gender on difficulties faced by entrepreneurs. *International Journal of Entrepreneurship and Innovation*, 5(3): 159–165.

Hersch, J. (2006) Sex discrimination in the labour market. *Foundations and Trends in Microeconomics*, 2(4): 281–361.

Hertz, L. (1986) *Business Amazons.* London: Deutsch.

Hilbrecht, M., Shaw, S., Johnson, L. and Andrey, J. (2008) I'm home for the kids: contradictory implications for work–life balance of teleworking mothers. *Gender, Work and Organization*, 15(5): 454–476.

Hill, F.M., Leitch, C.M. and Harrison, R. (2006) Desperately seeking finance? The demand for finance by women owned and led businesses. *Venture Capital*, 8(2): 159–182.

Hiralal, K. (2010) The invisible workers of the informal economy: a case study of home-based workers in Kwazulu/Natal, South Africa. *Journal of Social Science*, 23(1): 29–37.

Hirdman, Y. (1992) Utopia in the home. *International Journal of Political Economy*, 22(2): 5–99.

Hirdman, Y. (2001) *Genus – om det stabilas foranderliga* [Gender – changes of the Stable]. Stockholm: Liber AB.

Hisrich, R.D. (1985) The woman entrepreneur: characteristics, skills, problems and prescriptions for success. In D.L. Sexton and R.W Sailor (Eds), *The Art and Science of Entrepreneurship*. Cambridge, MA: Ballinger.

Hisrich, R.D. and Brush, C. (1986) *Women and Minority Entrepreneurs: A Comparative Analysis*. Working Paper. The University of Tulsa.

Hitt, M.A., Ireland, R.D., Camp, M. and Sexton, D.L. (2001) Strategic entrepreneurship: entrepreneurial strategies for wealth creation. *Strategic Management*, 22: 479–491.

Hjorth, D. and Steyeart, C. (Eds) (2004) *Narrative and Discursive Approaches in Entrepreneurship*. Cheltenham: Edward Elgar.

Hochschild, A. (1990) *The Second Shift*. New York: Avon Books.

Hofstede, G. (1980) Motivation, leadership and organisation: do American theories apply abroad? *Organisational Dynamics*, 9(1): 42–63.

Hollander, B.S. and Bukowitz, W.R. (1990) Women, family culture and family business. *Family Business Review*, 3(2): 139–151.

Holmes, J. (1997) Women, language and identity. *Journal of Sociolinguistics*, 1(2): 195–223.

Holmes, J. and Meyerhoff, M. (Eds) (2003) *The Handbook of Language and Gender*. Oxford: Blackwell.

Holmes, M. (2007) *What is Gender?* London: Sage.

Holmquist, C. and Sundin, E. (1988) Women as entrepreneurs in Sweden: conclusions from a survey. *Frontiers of Entrepreneurship Research*. Wellesley, MA: Babson College.

Holvino, E. (2010) Intersections: the simultaneity of race, gender and social class in organizations studies. *Gender, Work and Organization*, 17: 248–277.

hooks, b. (1981) *Ain't I a Woman: Black Women and Feminism*. Boston, MA: South End Press.

Howarth, C. and Assaraf Ali, Z. (2001) Family business succession in Portugal: an examination of case studies in the furniture industry. *Family Business Review*, 14(3): 231–244.

Hultin, M. (2003) Some take the glass escalator, some hit the glass ceiling? Career consequences of occupational sex segregation. *Work and Occupations*, 30(1): 30–61.

Hundley, G. (2000) Male/female earnings differences in self-employment: the effects of marriage, children and the household division of labour. *Industrial and Labour Relations Review,* 54: 95–114.

Hundley, G. (2001a) Why women earn less than men in self-employment. *Journal of Labour Research,* 22: 817–829.

Hundley, G. (2001b) Domestic division of labor and self/organisationally employed differences in job attitudes and earnings. *Journal of Family and Economic Issues,* 22(2): 121–139.

Hurley, A.E (1999) Incorporating feminist theories into sociological theories of entrepreneurship. *Women in Management Review,* 14(2): 54–62.

Hymowitz, C. and Schellhardt, T.D. (1986) The glass ceiling: why women can't break the invisible barrier that blocks them from top jobs. *Wall Street Journal,* March, 24(1): 5–10.

Ibarra, H. (1993) Personal networks of women and minorities in management: a conceptual framework. *Academy of Management Review,* 18(1): 56–88.

IFC-GEM (2006) *Middle East and North Africa (MENA) Regional Directory of Businesswomen's Associations.* New York: International Finance Corporation.

Ingraham, C. (2002) Heterosexuality: it's just not natural! In D. Richardson and S. Saidman (Eds), *Handbook of Lesbian and Gay Studies.* London: Sage.

IRiN (2011) *MIDDLE EAST: Refugees and IDPs by Country.* New York: UN Office for the Coordination of Humanitarian Affairs.

Jabre, B., Underwood, C. and Goodsmith, L. (1997) *Arab Women Speak Out: Profiles of Self-empowerment.* Baltimore, MD Johns Hopkins Centre for Communication Programs.

Jagose, A. (1996) *Queer Theory: An Introduction.* New York: New York University Books.

Jarvis, R. (2000) Finance and the small firm. In S. Carter and D. Jones (Eds), *Enterprise and Small Business: Principles, Practice and Policy.* London: Prentice Hall.

Jena, P.K. (2007) Orissan handicrafts in the age of globalization: challenges and opportunities. *Orissa Review,* LXIV (4): 19–25.

Jennings, J.E. and McDougald, M.S. (2007) Work–family interface experiences and coping strategies: implications for entrepreneurship research and practice. *The Academy of Management Review,* 32(3): 747–760.

Jones, O., Macpherson, A. and Thorpe, R. (2010) Promoting learning on owner-managed small firms: mediating artefacts and strategic space. *Entrepreneurship and Regional Development,* 22(7/8): 649–673.

Jones, S. (2011) *A Bourdieuian Approach to Researching HE Entrepreneurship Education and Gender.* Unpublished PhD Thesis: Leeds Metropolitan University, Leeds, UK.

Kalleberg, A.L. and Leicht, K.T. (1991) Gender and organizational performance: determinants of small business and success. *Academy of Management Journal,* 34(1): 136–161.

Kanazawa, S. (2005) Is discrimination necessary to explain the sex gap in earning? *Journal of Economics Psychology,* 26(2): 269–287.

Kanter, R.M. (1977) *Men and Women of the Corporation.* New York: Basic Books.

Kaplan, H. and Hill, K. (1985) Hunting ability and reproductive success among male Ache foragers. *Current Anthropology,* 26: 131–133.

Katungi, E., Edmeades, S. and Smale, M. (2008) Gender, social capital and information exchange in rural Uganda. *Journal of International Development,* 20(1): 35–52.

Kelan, E.K. (2009) Gender fatigue: the ideological dilemma of gender neutrality and discrimination in organisations. *Canadian Journal of Administrative Sciences,* 26: 197–210.

Kelan, E.K. (2010) Gender logic and (un)doing gender at work. *Gender, Work and Organization,* 17(2): 174–194.

Keltner, D. (1995) Signs of appeasement: evidence for the distinct displays of embarrassment, amusement and shame. *Journal of Personality and Social Psychology,* 68: 441–454.

Kepler, E. and Shane, S. (2007) *Are Male and Female Entrepreneurs Really that Different?* Washington, DC: US Small Business Administration, Office of Advocacy. Available at: http://www.sba.gov (retrieved 02.10.08).

Kepner, E. (1988) The family and the firm: a coevolutionary perspective. *Organisation Dynamics,* 12(1): 57–70.

Khawaja, M. and Tiltnes, A. (2002) *On the Margins: Migration and Living Conditions of Palestinian Camp Refugees in Jordan.* Norway: FAFO.

Klyver, K. and Terjesen, S. (2007) Entrepreneurial network composition: an analysis across venture development stage and gender. *Women in Management Review,* 22(8): 682–688.

Knights, D. and Kerfoot, D. (2004) Between representations and subjectivity: gender binaries and the politics of organizational transformation. *Gender, Work and Organization,* 11(4): 430–454.

Kon, Y. and Storey, D.J. (2003) A theory of discouraged borrowers. *Small Business Economics,* 21(1): 37–49.

Koss-Feder, L. (2001) Wife is boss in new business model for couples. *Women's eNews.* Available at: www.womensenews.org/article.cfm/dyn/aid/573/context/archive (c2002123) (accessed 15.11.09).

Krefting, L.A. (2009) Intertwined discourse of merit and gender: evidence from academic employment in the USA. *Gender, Work and Organisation,* 10: 260–278.

Kuratko, D. and Hodgetts, R. (1992) *Entrepreneurship: A Contemporary Approach.* New York: The Dryden Press.

Kuttab, D. (2008) *Sixty Years of the Palestinian Catastrophe.* Minivan News: Project Syndicate.

Kuttab, E. (2010) Empowerment as resistance: conceptualizing Palestinian women's empowerment. *Development,* 53(2): 247–253.

Landström, C. (2007) Queering feminist technology studies. *Feminist Theory*, 8(1): 7–26.

Langowitz, N. and Minniti, M. (2007) The entrepreneurial propensity of women. *Entrepreneurship Theory and Practice*, 31(3): 341–364.

Laure Humbert, A. (2012) *Women as Social Entrepreneurs*. Third Sector Research Centre Working Paper 72 TSRC.

Leavy, P. (2007) *Merging Feminist Principles and Arts-based Methodologies*. Paper presented at the meeting of the American Sociological Association, New York.

Lewis, K. and Massey, C. (2011) Critical yet invisible: the 'good wife' in the New Zealand small firm. *International Journal of Gender and Entrepreneurship*, 3(2): 105–122.

Lewis, P. (2006) The quest for invisibility: female entrepreneurs and their masculine norm of entrepreneurship. *Gender, Work and Organization*, 13(5): 453–469.

Lindh de Montoya, M. (2004) Driven entrepreneurs: a case study of taxi drivers in Caracas. In D. Hjorth and C. Steyeart (Eds), *Narrative and Discursive Approaches in Entrepreneurship*. Cheltenham: Edward Elgar.

Linehan, M. and Scullion, H. (2008) The development of female global managers: the role of mentoring and networking. *Journal of Business Ethics*, 83: 29–40.

Lippa, R.A. (2002) *Gender, Nature and Nurture*. Mahwah, NJ: Lawrence Erlbaum Associates.

Locke, E.A. (2000) Motivation, cognition and action: an analysis of studies of task goals and knowledge. *Applied Psychology: An International Review*, 49: 408–429.

Lucaccini, L.F. and Muscat, E.J. (2001) Family business and careers: classic and contemporary issues. *Career Planning and Adult Development Journal*, 17(2): 84–105.

McAdam, M. and Marlow, S. (2007) Building futures or stealing secrets? Entrepreneurial cooperation and conflict within business incubators. *International Journal of Small Business*, 25(4): 359–377.

McAdam, M. and Marlow, S. (2010) Constructing identities in the context of the business incubator: the challenges faced by the innovative female SET entrepreneur. In P. Wynarcyzk and S. Marlow (Eds), *Women, Innovation, Invention and Technology*. Bradford: ISBE/Emerald.

McAdam, M. and Marlow, S. (2012) Sectoral segregation or gendered practices? A case study of roles and identities in a copreneurial venture. In K.D. Hughes and J.E. Jennings (Eds), *Global Women's Entrepreneurship Research: Diverse Settings, Questions and Approaches*. Cheltenham: Edward Elgar.

McAdam, M. and Treanor, L. (2012) *An Investigation of the Discourses Surrounding Social Entrepreneurship Policy and Research: Is It Gendered?* Paper presented at Institute for Small Business and Entrepreneurship (ISBE) 2012 Annual Conference, Dublin, Ireland.

McGregor, J. and Tweed, D. (2002) Profiling a new generation of female small business owners in New Zealand: networking, mentoring and growth. *Gender, Work and Organisation*, 9(4): 420–438.

McKay, R. (2001) Women entrepreneurs: moving beyond family and flexibility. *International Journal of Entrepreneurial Behaviour*, 7(4): 148–165.

McKechnie, S.A., Ennew, C.T. and Read, L.H. (1998) The nature of the banking relationship: a comparison of the experiences of male and female small business owners. *International Small Business Journal*, 16(3): 39–55.

McMillan, C., O'Gorman, K. and MacLaren, A. (2011) Commercial hospitality: a vehicle for the sustainable empowerment of Nepali women. *International Journal of Contemporary Hospitality Management*, 23(2): 189–208.

Macran, S., Joshi, H. and Dex, S. (1996) Employment after childbearing: a survival analysis. *Work Employment and Society*, (10)2: 273–296.

McRobbie, A. (2009) *The Aftermath of Feminism*. London: Sage.

Mahoot, P. (1997) *Funding for Women Entrepreneurs: A Real, Though Disputed Problem*. Proceedings of the OECD Conference on Women Entrepreneurs in Small and Medium sized enterprises: A Major Force in Innovation and Job Creation, Paris.

Malhotra, A., Schuler, S.R. and Boender, C. (2002) *Measuring Women's Empowerment as a Variable in International Development*. Background Paper Prepared for the World Bank Workshop on Poverty and Gender: New Perspectives.

Mallon, M. and Cohen, L. (2001) Time for a change? Women's accounts of the move from organizational careers to self-employment. *British Journal of Management*, 12(3): 217–230.

Manolova, T.S., Carter, N.M., Manev, I.M. and Gyoshev, B.S. (2007) The differential effect of men and women entrepreneurs' human capital and networking on growth expectancies in Bulgaria. *Entrepreneurship, Theory and Practice*, 31(3): 407–426.

Marlow, M. and Carter, S. (2004) Accounting for change: professional status, gender disadvantage and self-employment. *Women in Management Review*, 19(1): 5–17.

Marlow, S. (1997) Self-employed women – new opportunities, old challenges? *Entrepreneurship and Regional Development*, 9(3): 199–210.

Marlow, S. (2002) Self-employed women: a part of or apart from feminist theory? *International Journal of Entrepreneurship and Innovation*, 2: 83–91.

Marlow, S. (2010) Perspectives in entrepreneurship: feminism, gender and entrepreneurship. In K. Mole and M. Ram (Eds), *Perspectives in Entrepreneurship: A Course Text*. London: Palgrave.

Marlow, S. and McAdam, M. (2011) Analyzing the influence of gender upon high-technology venturing within the context of business incubation. *Entrepreneurship, Theory and Practice*. DOI: 10.1111/j.1540-6520.2010.00431.x

Marlow, S. and McAdam, M. (2012) Gender and entrepreneurship: advancing debate and challenging myths – exploring the mystery of the under-performing female entrepreneur. *International Journal of Entrepreneurial Behaviour and Research*, forthcoming.

Marlow, S. and Patton, D. (2005) All credit to men? Entrepreneurship, finance and gender. *Entrepreneurship, Theory and Practice*, 29: 717–735.

REFERENCES

Marlow, S. and Strange, A. (1994) Female Entrepreneurs – success by whose standards? In M. Tanton (Ed.), *Women in Management: A Developing Presence*. London: Routledge.

Marlow, S., Carter, S. and Shaw, E. (2008) Constructing female entrepreneurship policy in the UK: is the US a relevant benchmark? *Environment and Planning C: Government and Policy*, 26: 335–351.

Marlow, S., Henry, C. and Carter, S. (2009) Exploring the impact of gender upon women's business ownership. *International Small Business Journal*, 27(2): 139–148.

Marshack, K. (1993) Copreneurial couples: a literature review on boundaries and transitions among copreneurs. *Family Business Review*, 6(4): 355–369.

Marshack, K. (1994) Copreneurs and dual-career couples: are they different? *Entrepreneurship Theory and Practice*, 19(1): 49–69.

Marshack, K. (1998) *Entrepreneurial Couples: Making It Work at Work and at Home*. Palo Alto, CA: Davies-Black.

Martin, L. (2001) Are women better at organisational learning? An SME perspective. *Women in Management Review*, 16(5–6): 287–296.

Martin, P.Y. (2003) 'Said and done' versus 'saying and doing' – gendering practices, practising gender at work. *Gender and Society*, 17(3): 342–366.

Martinez Jimenez, R. (2009) Research on women in family: current status and future directions. *Family Business Review*, 22(1): 53–64.

Mason, C.M. and Harrison, R.T. (1992) The supply of equity finance in the UK: a strategy for closing the equity gap. *Entrepreneurship and Regional Development*, 4: 357–380.

Mason, C.M. and Harrison, R.T. (1999) Public policy and the development of the informal venture capital market: UK experience and lessons for Europe. In K. Cowling (Ed.), *Industrial Policy in Europe* (pp. 199–223). London: Routledge.

Mason, C.M. and Harrison, R.T. (2000) The size of the informal venture capital market in the UK. *Small Business Economics*, 15: 137–148.

Mayer, H. (2006) Economic trends and location patterns of women high-tech entrepreneurs. In A. Zacharakis *et al.* (Eds), *Frontiers of Entrepreneurship Research*. Wellesley, MA: Babson College.

Meager, N., Bates, P. and Cowling, M. (2003) An evaluation of business start-up support for young people. *National Institute Economic Review*, 186(1): 59–72.

Meagher, K. (2010) The empowerment trap: gender, poverty and the informal economy in sub-Saharan Africa. In S. Chant (Ed.), *The International Handbook of Gender and Poverty: Concepts, Research, Policy* (pp. 472–477). Cheltenham: Edward Elgar.

Mehra, R. (1997) Women, empowerment, and economic development. *The Annals of the Academy*, 554: 136–149.

Merriman, R. (2007) Palestinian refugees and exiles must have a say-so. *The Electronic Intifada*. Available at: http://noiivan.blogspot.com/2007_01_01_archive.html (accessed 28.06.08).

Mills, M. and Voerman, J.A. (1997) *Female and Male Entrepreneurs in Sweden and the Netherlands: A Test of Liberal and Social Feminism*. Paper presented at the RENT-XI Conference, Mannheim.

Minniti, M. (2009) Gender issues in entrepreneurship. *Foundations and Trends in Entrepreneurship*, 5(7–8): 497–621.

Minniti, M. and Arenius, P. (2003) *Women in Entrepreneurship*. Paper presented at the Entrepreneurial Advantage of Nations: First Annual Global Entrepreneurship Symposium, United Nations Headquarters, 29 April 2003.

Minniti, M., Arenius, P. and Langowitz, N. (2005) *2004 Global Entrepreneurship Monitor Special Topic Report: Women and Entrepreneurship*. Center for Women's Leadership at Babson College, Babson Park, MA.

Mirchandani, K. (1999) Feminist insight on gendered work: new directions in research on women and entrepreneurship. *Gender, Work and Organization*, 6(4): 224–235.

Mirchandani, K. (2005) Women's entrepreneurship: exploring new avenues. In S. Fielden and M. Davidson (Eds), *International Handbook of Women and Small Business Entrepreneurship*. London: Edward Elgar.

Molyneux, M. (2006) Mothers at the service of the new poverty agenda: PROGRESA/ Oportunidades, Mexico's conditional transfer programme. *Journal of Social Policy and Administration*, 40(4): 425–449.

Monaci, M. (1997) *Genere e Organizzazione*. Milan: Guerini e Associtai.

Monaghan, L.F. (2002) Hard men, shop boys and others: embodying competence in a masculinist occupation. *The Sociologist Review*, 50: 334–355.

Moore, D.P. and Buttner, E.H. (1997) *Women Entrepreneurs: Moving Beyond the Glass Ceiling*. Thousand Oaks, CA: Sage.

Morris, M.H., Miyasaki, N.H., Watters, C.E. and Coombes, S.M. (2006) The dilemma of growth: understanding venture size choice of women entrepreneurs. *Journal of Small Business Management*, 44(2): 221–244.

Morrison, A.M., White, R.P., Van Velsor, E. and the Center for Creative Leadership (1987) *Breaking the Glass Ceiling: Can Women Reach the Top of America's Largest Corporations?* Reading, MA: Addison-Wesley.

Mosedale, S. (2005) Assessing women's empowerment: towards a conceptual framework. *Journal of International Development*, 17(2): 243–257.

Moult, S. and Anderson, A.R. (2005) Enterprising women: gender and maturity in new venture creation and development. *Journal of Enterprising Culture*, 13(3): 255–271.

Mulholland, K. (1996) Gender and the property relations within entrepreneurial wealthy families. *Gender Work and Organisation*, 3(2): 78–102.

Myers, S.C. (1984) The capital structure puzzle. *The Journal of Finance*, 39(3): 575–572. Papers and Proceedings, Forty-Second Annual Meeting, American Finance Association, July.

Nadin, S. (2007) Entrepreneurial identity in the care sector: navigating the contradictions. *Women in Management Review*, 22: 456–67.

REFERENCES

Nahapiet, J. and Ghoshal, S. (1998) Social capital, intellectual capital, and the organisational advantage. *Academy of Management Review*, 23(2): 242–266.

Narain, S. and Morse, J. (2008) *Gender, Social Capital and the Development Discourse: A Critical Perspective*. UCLA Centre for the Study of Women: Thinking Gender Papers, University of California, Los Angeles.

Narayan, D., Patel, R., Schafft, K., Rademacher, A. and Koch-Schulte, S. (2000) *Voices of the Poor: Can Anyone Hear Us?* World Bank Series, Oxford: Oxford University Press.

Naude, W.A. and Van der Walt, L. (2008) Opportunity or necessity? The spatial determinants of entrepreneurship in South Africa. *International Journal of Entrepreneurship and Small Business*, 3(2): 245–265.

Neergaard, H. Frederiksen, S. and Marlow, S. (2011) *The Emperor's New Clothes: Rendering a Feminist Theory of Entrepreneurship Visible*. Paper to the 56th ICSB Conference, June, Stockholm.

Nosek, B.A., Smyth, F.L., Sriram, N., Lindner, N.M., Devos, T. and Ayala, A. (2009) National differences in gender–science stereotypes predict national sex differences in science and math achievement. *Proceedings of the National Academy of Sciences*, 106(26): 10593–10597.

Oakley, A. (1972) *Sex, Gender and Society*. London: Temple Smith.

Oakley, J.G. (2000) Gender-based barriers to senior management positions: understanding the scarcity of female CEOs. *Journal of Business Ethics*, 27(4): 321–334.

Ogbor, J. (2000) Mythicizing and reification in entrepreneurial discourse: ideology-critique of entrepreneurship studies. *Journal of Management Studies*, 37(5): 605–635.

O'Reilly, M. (2004) *The Position of Women in the Economy: A Baseline Analysis*. Economic Research Institute of Northern Ireland, NI.

Orhan, M. (2001) Women business owners in France: the issue of financing discrimination. *Journal of Small Business Management*, 39(1): 95–102.

Orser, B.J., Riding, A.L. and Manley, K. (2005) Equity and equity: application and approval for financing women-owned Canadian SMEs. *Proceedings, Administrative Science Association of Canada, Ryerson Polytechnic University*, Toronto, 28–31 May.

Osberg, S. and Martin, R. (2007) Social entrepreneurship: the case for definition. *Stanford Social Innovation Review*, Spring: 28–39.

Panteli, A., Ramsey, H. and Beirne, M. (1997) *Engendered Systems Development: Ghettoization and Agency*. International IFIP Conference, Women Work and Computerization: Spinning a Web from Past to Future, Bonn, 24–27 May.

Panteli, N., Stack, J. and Ramsay, H. (2001) Gendered patterns in computing work in the later 1990s. *New Technology, Work and Employment*, 16(1): 3–16.

Parker, S.C. (2009) *The Economics of Entrepreneurship*. Cambridge: Cambridge University Press.

Patterson, N. and Mavin, S. (2009) Women entrepreneurs: jumping the corporate ship and gaining new wings. *International Small Business Journal*, 27(2): 173–192.

Pepelasis Minoglou, I. (2007) Women and family capitalism in Greece, *c.* 1780–1940. *Business History Review*, 81(3): 517–538.

Perrons, D. (2004) *Globalisation and Social Change: People and Places in a Divided World*. London: Routledge.

Philbrick, C.A. and Fitzgerald, M.A. (2007) Women in business-owning families: a comparison of roles, responsibilities and predictors of family functionality. *Journal of Family and Economic Issues*, 28(4): 618–634.

Pini, B. (2005) The third sex: women leaders in australian agriculture. *Gender Work and Organisation*, 12: 73–88.

Pinson, L. and Jinnett, J. (1992) *The Woman Entrepreneur: 33 Personal Stories of Success*. Dover: Upstart Publishing Company.

Polanyi, K. (1957) *The Great Transformation: The Political and Economic Origin of our Time*. Boston: Beacon Hill.

Portes, A. (1998) Social capital: its origins and applications in modern sociology. *Annual Review of Sociology*, 24: 1–24.

Powell, G.N. and Butterfield, D.A. (1994) Investigating the 'glass ceiling' phenomenon: an empirical study of actual promotions to top management. *Academy of Management Journal*, 37(1): 68–86.

Poza, E. and Messer, T. (2001) Spousal leadership and continuity in the family firm. *Family Business Review*, 14(1): 25–36.

Prowess (2003) *Prowess Best Practice Report*. Prowess, UK.

Puhakka, V. (2002) *Entrepreneurial Business Opportunity Recognition: Relationships Between Intellectual and Social Capital, Environmental Dynamism, Opportunity Recognition Behaviour, and Performance*. Doctoral dissertation, University of Oulu, Finland.

Putnam, R. (1993) *Making Democracy Work: Civic Traditions in Modern Italy*. Princeton, NJ: Princeton University Press.

Putnam, R. (1995) Bowling alone: America's declining social capital. *Journal of Democracy*, 6: 65–78.

QSR (2008) http://www.qsrinternational.com/support_faqs_detail.aspx?view=358

Radu, M. and Redien-Collot, R. (2008) The social representation of entrepreneurs in the french press: desirable and feasible models? *International Small Business Journal*, 26(3): 259–298.

Rake, K., Davies, H., Joshi, H. and Alami, R. (2000) *Women's Incomes over the Lifetime*. A report to the Women's Unit, Cabinet Office.

Ram, M. and Holliday, R. (1983) Relative merits: family culture and kinship in small firms. *Sociology*, 27(4): 629–648.

Ramussen, S. (2005) Tuareg diaspora. In M. Ember, C. Ember and I. Skoggard (Eds), *Encyclopedia of Diasporas* (pp. 309–318). Los Angeles: Springer US.

Rand, T.M. and Wexley, K.N. (1975) Demonstration of the effect 'similar to me' in simulated employment interviews. *Psychological Reports,* 36: 535–544.

Ranga, M. and Etzkowitz, H. (2010) Athena in the world of techne: the gender dimension of technology, innovation and entrepreneurship. *Journal of Technology Management and Innovation,* 5(1): 3–11.

Reinharz, S. (1992) *Feminist Methods in Social Research.* Oxford: Oxford University Press.

Renzulli, L.A., Aldrich, H. and Moody, J. (2000) Family matters: gender, family, and entrepreneurial outcomes. *Social Forces,* 79(2): 523–546.

Reynolds, P.D., Bygrave, W.D., Autio, E., Cox, L. and Hay, M. (2002), *Global Entrepreneurship Monitor: 2002 Executive Report.* Kansas City, MO: Kauffman Center for Entrepreneurial Leadership.

Reynolds, P.D., Bygrave, W. and Autio, E. (2004) *GEM 2003 Executive Report.* Babson Park, MA: Babson College; London, UK: London Business School and Kansa City, MO: Kauffman Foundation.

Ridgeway, C.L. (1997) Interaction and the conservation of gender inequality: considering employment. *American Sociological Review,* 62(2): 218–235.

Riding, A. and Swift, C. (1990) Women business owners and terms of credit: some empirical findings of the Canadian experience. *Journal of Business Venturing,* 5(5): 327–340.

Rindova, V., Barry, D. and Ketchen, D. (2009) Entrepreneuring as emancipation. *Academy of Management Review,* 34(3): 477–491.

Roodman, D. and Morduch, J. (2009) The Impact of Micro Credit on the Poor in Bangladesh, Working Paper no. 174. Technical Report: Center for Global Development, New York University.

Roper, S. and Scott, J.M. (2007) Gender differences in access to start-up finance: an econometric analysis of GEM data. Institute of Small Business and Entrepreneurship Conference (ISBE), Glasgow, November 2007.

Rosa, P., Carter, S. and Hamilton, D. (1996) Gender as a determinant of small business performance: insights from a British study. *Small Business Economics,* 8(6): 463–478.

Rosenblatt, P.C., de Mik, L., Anderson, R.M. and Johnson, P.A. (1985) *The Family in Business.* San Francisco, CA: Jossey-Bass.

Rosenbloom, J.L., Ash, R.A., Dupont, B. and Coer, L. (2008) Why are there so few women in information technology? Assessing the role of personality in career choice. *Journal of Economic Psychology,* 29: 543–554.

Roseneil, S. (2000) Queer frameworks and queer tendencies: towards an understanding of post modern transformations of sexuality. *Sociological Research Online,* 5(3). Available at: http://www.socresonline.org.uk/5/3roseneil.html

Rouse, J. and Kitching, J. (2006) Do enterprise programmes leave women holding the baby? *Environmental Planning C: Government and Policy,* 24(1): 5–19.

Rowe, B.R. and Bentley, M.T. (1992) The impact of the family on home-based work. *Journal of Family and Economic Issues*, 13: 279–297.

Rowe, B.R. and Hong, G.S. (2000) The role of wives in family businesses: the paid and unpaid work of women. *Family Business Review*, 13: 1–13.

Ruef, M., Aldrich, H.E. and Carter, N.M. (2003) The structure of founding partnerships: homophily, strong ties, and isolation among US entrepreneurs. *American Sociological Review*, 68(2): 195–222.

Salganicoff, M. (1990) Women in family business: challenges and opportunities. *Family Business Review*, 3(2): 125–137.

Sandberg, W.R. (1986) *New Venture Performance*. Lexington, MA: D.C. Heath and Co.

Sardenberg, C. (2008) Liberal vs. liberating empowerment: a Latin American feminist perspective on conceptualising women's empowerment. *IDS Bulletin*, 39(6): 18–27.

Scherer, R., Brodzinski, J. and Wiebe, F.A. (1990) Entrepreneurship career selection and gender: a socialisation approach. *Journal of Small Business Management*, 28(2): 37–44.

Schwartz, E.B. (1976) Entrepreneurship: a new female frontier. *Journal of Contemporary Business*, Winter: 47–76.

Scott, C.E. (1986) Why more women are becoming entrepreneurs. *Journal of Small Business Management*, 24(4): 37–45.

Scott-Dixon, K. (2004) *Doing It: Women working in Information Technology*. Toronto: Sumach Press.

Sexton, D.L. and Bowman-Upton, N. (1990) Female and male entrepreneurs: psychological characteristics and their role in gender related discrimination. *Journal of Business Venturing*, 5(1): 29–36.

Shabbir, A. and di Gregorio, S. (1996) An examination of the relationship between women's personal goals and structural factors influencing their decision to start a business: the case of Pakistan. *Journal of Business Venturing*, 11(6): 507–529.

Shanahan, S. and Tuma, N. (1994) The sociology of distribution and redistribution. In N. Smelser and R. Swedberg (Eds), *The Handbook of Economic Sociology* (pp. 733–765). Princeton, NJ and New York: Princeton University Press and Russell Sage Foundation.

Shane, S., Locke, E. and Collins, C. (2003) Entrepreneurial motivation. *Human Resource Management Review*, 13(2): 257–279.

Sharma, P. (2004) An overview of the field of family business studies: current status and directions for the future. *Family Business Review*, 17: 1–36.

Shaw, E. (2003) Marketing through alliances and networks. In S. Hart (Ed.), *Marketing Changes* (pp. 147–170). London: Thomson Learning.

Shaw, E. (2006) Small firm networking: an insight into contents and motivating factors. *International Small Business Journal*, 24(1): 5–30.

Shaw, E., Carter, S. and Brierton, J. (2001) *Unequal Entrepreneur: Why Female Enterprise is an Uphill Business.* The Work Foundation, The Industrial Society Policy Paper, October, pp. 1–19.

Shaw, E., Carter, S., Lam, W. and Wilson, F. (2005) *Social Capital and Accessing Finance: The Relevance of Networks.* Paper presented at the 28th Institute for Small Business and Entrepreneurship, Blackpool.

Shelton, L.M. (2006) Female entrepreneurs, work–family conflict, and venture performance: new insights into the work–family interface. *Journal of Small Business Management,* 44(2): 285–297.

Sholkamy, H. (2010) Power, politics and development in the Arab context: or how can rearing chicks change patriarchy? *Development,* 53(2): 254–258.

Small Business Service (2003) *A Strategic Framework for Women's Enterprise.* London: Small Business Service. Available at: http://www.prowess.org.uk/pdfs/strageic%20framework.pdf

Smallbone, D. and Wyer, P. (2006) Growth and development in the small business. In S. Carter and D. Jones-Evans (Eds), *Enterprise and Small Business: Principles, Practice and Policy.* Harlow: Pearson Education.

Smith, C.R. (2000) Managing work and family in small copreneurial business: an Australian study. *Women in Management Review,* 15(5/6): 283–289.

Smith, E. and Bird, D. (2001) The hunting handicap: costly signaling in human foraging strategies. *Behavioral Ecology and Sociobiology,* 50: 9–19.

Smith, R. and Anderson, A.R. (2004) The Devil is in the E-tail: forms and structures in the entrepreneurial narratives. In D. Hjorth and C. Steyaert (Eds), *Narrative and Discursive Approaches in Entrepreneurship* (pp. 125–143). Cheltenham: Edward Elgar.

Smyth, C. (2010) Equal pay for women half a century away. *The Times,* 19 August: 19.

Sommerlad, H. and Sanderson, P. (1998) *Gender, Choice and Commitment.* Aldershot: Ashgate.

Sonfield, M., Lussier, R., Corman, J. and McKinney, M. (2001) Gender comparisons in strategic decision making: an empirical analysis of the entrepreneurial strategy mix. *Journal of Small Business Management,* 39(2): 165–172.

Starr, J. and Yudkin, M. (1996) *Women Entrepreneurs: A Review of Current Research.* Wellesley, MA: Wellesley College Center for Research on Women.

Steele, C.M., Spencer, S.J. and Aronson, J. (2002) Contending with group image: the psychology of stereotype and social identity threat. In M.P. Zanna (Ed.), *Advances in Experimental Social Psychology.* San Diego, CA: Elsevier, vol. 34.

Steier, L. and Greenwood, R. (2000) Entrepreneurship and the evolution of angel financial networks. *Organization Studies,* 21(1): 163–192.

Stevenson, L. (1990) Some methodological problems associated with researching women entrepreneurs. *Journal of Business Ethics,* 9(4): 439–446.

Stewart-Gross, B.L. and Gross, M. (2007) *Sleeping with our Business Partner: A Communication Toolkit for Couples in Business Together.* Washington DC: Capital Books.

Steyaert, C. (2007) Entrepreneuring as conceptual attractor? A review of process theories in 20 years of entrepreneurship studies. *Entrepreneurship and Regional Development*, 19(4): 453–477.

Steyaert, C. and Katz, J. (2004) Reclaiming the space of entrepreneurship in society: geographical, discursive and social dimensions. *Entrepreneurship and Regional Development*, 16: 179–196.

Still, L.V. and Walker, E.A. (2006) The self-employed woman owner and her business: an Australian profile. *Women in Management Review*, 21(4): 294–310.

Stinchcombe, A.L. (1965) Social structures and organizations. In J.G. March (Ed.), *Handbook of Organizations* (pp. 142–193). Chicago: Rand McNally.

Storey, D. (1994) *Understanding the Small Firm Sector*. London: Routledge.

Sundin, E. (1988) Osynliggörandet av kvinnor – exemplet företagare. *Kvinnovetenskaplig tidskrift*, 9(1): 3–15.

Tabbaa, Y. (2010) Female Labour Force Participation in Jordan, Economic and Social Council Policy Papers, Amman – Jordan. Available at: http://esc.jo/en/female-labour-force-participation-jordan (accessed December 2010).

Taylor, S. and Marlow, S. (2009) *Engendering Entrepreneurship: Why Can't a Women be More Like a Man?* Paper presented at the 26th EURAM Conference, Liverpool.

Teasdale, S., McKay, S., Phillimore, J. and Teasdale, N. (2011) Exploring gender and social entrepreneurship: women's leadership, employment and participation in the third sector and social enterprises. *Voluntary Sector Review*, 2(1): 57–76.

Teece, D.J. (2011) Human capital, capabilities and the firm: literati, numerati and entrepreneurs in the twenty-first century enterprise. In A. Burton-Jones and J.-C. Spender (Eds), *The Oxford Handbook of Human Capital*. Oxford: Oxford University Press.

Thompson, P., Jones-Evans, D. and Kwong, C. (2009) Women and home based entrepreneurship: evidence from the United Kingdom. *International Small Business Journal*, 27(2): 227–237.

Timberlake, S. (2005) Social capital and gender in the workplace. *Journal of Management Development*, 24(1): 34–44.

Tompson, G.H. and Tompson, H.B. (2000) *Determinants of Successful Copreneurship*. Paper presented at ICSB World Conference Brisbane, Australia.

Trauth, E.M. (2002) Odd girl out: an individual differences perspective on women in the ICT profession. *Information and Technology and People*, 15(2): 98–118.

Turk, T.A. and Shelton, L. (2004) Growth aspirations, risk, gender and legal form: a look at the services industries. *Academy of Entrepreneurship Journal*, 12(1): 35–46.

Turner, A. (2010) They know the way to the top. *The Sunday Times*, 14 March: 7.

UNIFEM (2004) *Progress of Arab Women*. Amman: UNIFEM.

US Census Bureau (2002) Historical income tables – full-time year-round workers by median income and sex, 1995 to 2001. Available at http://www.census.gov

Uzzi, B. (1997) Social structures and competition in interfirm networks: the paradox of embeddedness. *Administrative Science Quarterly*, 42: 35–67.

Vallianatos, H. and Raine, K. (2007) Reproducing home: Arab women's experiences of Canada. *Al-Raida*, 24(116–117): 35–51.

Van Auken, H., Gaskill, L. and Kao, S. (1993) Acquisition of capital by women entrepreneurs: patterns of initial and refinancing capitalisation. *Journal of Small Business and Entrepreneurship*, 10(4): 44–55.

Van der Lippe, T. and van Dijk, L. (2002) Comparative research on women's employment. *Annual Review of Sociology*, 28: 221–241.

van Doorn-Harder, N. (2011) Egypt: does the revolution include the Copts?' *Open Democracy*. Available at: http://www.opendemocracy.net/5050/nelly-van-doorn-harder/egypt-does-revolution-include-copts

Veil, S. (1994) Allocution d'ouverture, Actes du Colloque Europeen du Janvier 1994. *Femmes Argent Enterprise*, 9–14.

Vera, C.F. and Dean, M.A. (2005) An examination of the challenges daughters face in family business succession. *Family Business Review*, 18(4): 321–345.

Verheul, I. and Thurik, R. (2001) Start-up capital: does gender matter? *Small Business Economics*, 16(4): 329–345.

Verheul, I., van Stel, A. and Thurik, R. (2004) *Explaining Male and Female Entrepreneurship Across 29 Countries*. Netherlands: EIM Business and Policy Research.

Wacquant, L. (1993) On the tracks of symbolic power: prefatory notes to Bourdieu's states of nobility. *Theory, Culture and Society*, 10: 1–17.

Wajcman, J. (1991) *Feminism Confronts Technology*. Oxford: Policy Press.

Wajcman, J. (2004) *Technofeminism*. Cambridge: Polity Press.

Wajcman, J. and Wilson, F. (2003) Can compute, won't compute: women's participation in the culture of computing. *New Technology, Work and Employment*, 18(2): 127–142.

Walby, S., Gottfried, H., Gottschall, K. and Osawa, M. (2007) *Gendering the Knowledge Economy: Comparative Perspectives*. Houndmills/Basingstoke: Palgrave.

Warren, T., Rowlingson, K. and Whyley, C. (2001) Female finances: gender wage gaps and gender assets gaps. *Work, Employment and Society*, (15)3: 465–488.

Watkins, D. and Watkins (1986) The female entrepreneurs: her background and determinants of business choice – some British data. In J. Curran, J. Stanworth and D. Watkins (Eds), *The Survival of the Small Firm* (pp. 220–232). Aldershot: Gower.

Watson, J. (2002) Comparing the performance of male and female controlled businesses: relating outputs to inputs. *Entrepreneurship, Theory and Practice*, 26(3): 91–100.

Watson, J. (2003) Failure rates for female controlled businesses: are they any different? *Journal of Small Business Management*, 41(3): 262–277.

Watson, J. and Robinson, S. (2003) Adjusting for risk in comparing the performance of male- and female-controlled SMEs. *Journal of Business Venturing*, 18: 773–784.

Watts, J.H. (2007) Porn, pride and pessimism: experiences of women working in professional construction roles. *Work, Employment and Society*, 21(2): 299–316.

Weatherall, A. (2002) *Gender, Language and Discourse*. London: Routledge.

Weeks, J. (2009) Women business owners in the Middle East and North Africa: a five-country research study. *International Journal of Gender and Entrepreneurship*, 1(1): 77–85.

Weiler, S. and Bernasek, A. (2001) Dodging the glass ceiling? Networks and the new wave of women entrepreneurs. *Social Science Journal*, 38: 85–105.

Welter, F. (2004) The environment for female entrepreneurships in Germany. *Journal of Small Business and Enterprise Development*, 11(2): 212–221.

Welter, F. (2011) Contextualising entrepreneurship – conceptual challenges and ways forward. *Entrepreneurship, Theory and Practice*, 35(1): 165–184.

Welter, F. and Smallbone, S. (2008) Women's entrepreneurship from an institutional perspective: the case of Uzbekistan. *International Entrepreneurship and Management Journal*, 4(4): 505–520.

Welter, F. and Smallbone, D. (2010) Women's entrepreneurship in a transition context. In C. Brush, E. Gatewood, C. Henry and A. de Bruin (Eds), *Women's entrepreneurship and Growth Influences*. London: Edward Elgar.

West, C. and Zimmerman, D.H. (1987) Doing gender. *Gender and Society*, 1(2): 125–151.

Westhead, P., Wright, M. and McElwee, E. (2011) *Entrepreneurship: Perspectives and Cases*. London: FT Prentice Hall.

Whetton, D. A. (1989) What constitutes a theoretical contribution? *Academy of Management Review*, 14(4): 490–495.

Whitehead, S. (2008) *Men and Masculinities*. London: Polity Press.

Wijbenga, F. and Postma, T. (2007) The influence of venture capitalist's governance activities on the entrepreneurial firm's control system and performance. *Entrepreneurship, Theory and Practice*, 31(2): 257–277.

Williams, C. (1992) The glass escalator: hidden advantages for men in the 'female' professions. *Social Problems*, 39(3): 253–267.

Williams, C. (1993) *Doing 'Women's Work': Men in Non-traditional Occupations*. Newbury Park, CA: Sage.

Williams, C. (2004) The glass escalator: hidden advantages for men in the female profession. In M.S. Kimmel and M.A. Messner (Eds), *Men's Lives* (pp. 227–239). Boston: Pearson.

Wilson, B.C. (2002) A study of factors promoting success in computer science including gender differences. *Computer Science Education*, 12(1–2): 141–164.

Wingfield, A. (2009) Racializing the glass escalator: reconsidering men's experiences with women's work. *Gender and Society*, 23(1): 5–26.

Women and Equality Unit (2008) *Working and Living*. Available at: http://www.women andequalityunit.gov.uk/work_life/index.htm www.ukbi.co.uk

Women and Work Commission (2006) *Shaping a Fairer Future*. London: Women and Equality Unit, DTI.

Woodfield, R. (2002) Women and information systems development: not just a pretty (inter)face? *Information Technology and People*, 15(2): 119–137.

Woolcook, M. (1998) Social capital and economic development: towards a theoretical synthesis and policy framework. *Theory and Society*, 27: 151–208.

World Bank (2006) *Data and Statistics: Labour and Employment, World Development Indicators*. Available at: http://www.worldbank.org

World Bank (2010) *World Development Indicators 2010*. Washington DC: World Bank Group.

Wright, S.C. (1997) Ambiguity, social influence, and collective action: generating collective protest in response to tokenism. *Personality and Social Psychology Bulletin*, 23: 1277–1290.

Wynarczyk, P. (2009) Providing the science, technology, engineering and mathematics skills of tomorrow. *New Technology, Work and Employment*, 24(3): 243–259.

Wynarczyk, P. and Renner, C. (2006) The 'gender gap' in the scientific labour market: the case of science, engineering and technology-based SMEs in the UK. *Equal Opportunities International*, 25(8): 660–673.

www.queenrania.jo (27 June 2008).

Young, M. and Willmott, P. (1973) *The Symmetrical Family: A Study of Work and Leisure in the London Region*. London: Routledge and Kegan Paul.

Zablocki, B.D. and Kanter, R.M. (1976) The differentiation of life-styles. *Annual Review of Sociology*, 2: 269–298.

Zhao, H.S., Seibert, S.E. and Hills, G.E. (2005) The mediating role of self-efficacy in the development of entrepreneurial intentions. *Journal of Applied Psychology*, 90: 1265–1272.

Index

3M model, 44
5M model, 44–46

adaptive women, 14–16
Ahl, H.J., 1, 37, 95–96, 104
Arab women, entrepreneurial emancipation study: background, 79, 83–85; cultural influences, 87–89, 100; empowerment indicators, 90–92; gendered division of labour, 87–88; political engagement, 89–90; study method, 84–87
Ashcraft, K.L., 42

Bem, S.L., 23–24
Bjorkman, C., 75
Bourdieu, P., 54
Bruce, D., 45
Brush, C.G., 1, 39, 45, 66, 68
business angels, 67–68, 101–102
business finance *see* entrepreneurial capital
business performance: cultural influences, 45–46; economic influences, 29; failure, focus on, 27–29; models of, 45–46
business sectors *see also* science, engineering and technology: gender typical preferences, 4–5, 9–10, 26–29; socio-economic positioning, 16–17, 29, 64, 83, 96, 105–107
business size, 28–29
Butler, J., 32–33, 38
Bygrave, W.D., 66

capital, financial: access restrictions, 61–62, 64–69, 101–102; bank finance, 64–65; business angels, 67–68, 101–102; debt risk

aversion, 63, 65–66; financial credibility, 62–63; gender, influence of, 55, 61–65; micro-funding, 101–102; pecking order hypothesis, 63–64; pipeline effect, 63–64, 72–73, 77; research trends, 101–102; start-up capital, 61–62; stereotypes, influence of, 65, 68–69; venture capital, 66–69, 101–102
capital, non-financial: definition, 53–54; experience, role of, 60; gender influences, 53–54; human capital, 54–55; social capital, 55–56; symbolic capital, 59–60; undercapitalisation, 11, 53–54
carers, 9–10, 65; *see also* childcare
Chant, S., 79–80, 82, 90–91
childcare: entrepreneurship, influence on, 5–6, 43–45; institutional constraints, 17; parenthood styles, gender influences, 11–12; preference theory, 14–16; responsibilities for, 11–12, 45; secondary nature of, 96; and women's place in labour market, 9, 41–43, 45–46
class, relevance of, 1–2
contraception, 14
coping strategies, 36, 75, 77
copreneurs: business trends, 49–50; division of labour, 50–52
Cruikshank, Lilias, 56
culture: and business performance, 45–46; contextual role, 79–81, 83–84, 87–89, 100–101; entrepreneurial empowerment through, 79, 87–92; and gender stereotypes, 23–25, 32; relevance of, 1–2; vertical segregation, 10